Many Faces,
One Church

A Manual for Cross-Racial and Cross-Cultural Ministry

ERNEST S. LYGHT
GLORY E. DHARMARAJ
JACOB S. DHARMARAJ

Abingdon Press
Nashville

MANY FACES, ONE CHURCH
A MANUAL FOR CROSS-RACIAL AND CROSS-CULTURAL MINISTRY

This book is printed on acid-free paper.

Library of Congress Cataloging-in-Publication Data

Lyght, Ernest S., 1934-
    Many faces, one church : a manual for cross-racial and cross-cutural ministry / Ernest S. Lyght, Glory E. Dharmaraj, Jacob S. Dharmaraj.
        p. cm.
    Includes bibliographical references.
    ISBN 0-687-49445-1 (binding: pbk. : alk. paper)
    1. United Methodist Church (U.S.)—Clergy—Appointment, call, and election.   2. Methodist Church—Clergy—Appointment, call, and election.   3. Race—Religious aspects—Methodist Church.   4. Ethnicity—Religious aspects—Methodist Church.   5. Cultural relations.   I. Dharmaraj, Glory E., 1945-   II. Dharmaraj, Jacob S.   III. Title.

BX8389.5.L94 2006
287'.6089—dc22
ISBN 13: 978-0-687-49445-3   2005032033

All scripture quotations (unless noted otherwise) are take from the *New Revised Standard Version of the Bible*, copyright © 1989, by the Division of Christian Education of the National Council of the Churches of Christ in the United States of America. Used by permission. All rights reserved.

Scripture quotations marked KJV are from the King James or Authorized Version of the Bible.

Quotations from the *Discipline* are from *The Book of Discipline of The United Methodist Church 2004* © 2004 by The United Methodist Publishing House.

08 09 10 11 12 13 14 15—10 9 8 7 6 5 4 3

MANUFACTURED IN THE UNITED STATES OF AMERICA

CONTENTS

Part III—*What?* Resources for Ministry

PREFACE

The preparation of persons for the work of ministry in The United Methodist Church actually begins in the local congregation and culminates with the Annual Conference Board of Ordained Ministry. It is useful for a person who is responding to God's call to ministry to be nurtured by one's congregation. Such congregational nurture is a crucial dimension in a pastor's journey into ministry. The congregation plays a critical role in developing persons as leaders, particularly as pastoral leaders. It is within the context of the congregation that a person can participate actively in spiritual nurture, biblical education, Christian fellowship, and leadership development.

Young women and men begin learning about leadership by observing lay and pastoral leadership in the congregations where they are nurtured in the Christian faith. Children generally thrive in an atmosphere where the adult leadership and church school teachers around them encourage creativity, inquisitiveness, and risk-taking. Moreover, leadership begins to take root with group participation and interaction, such as joining a youth group, Sunday school class, choir, dance troupe, or Bible study fellowship.

Typically, these groups provide opportunities for young people to learn about the reality and dimensions of leadership. By serving as the president of a youth group, a choir, or other group, young people gain practical experience in leadership, which is invaluable to a person responding to God's call to ministry.

Within the congregation, the Staff-Parish Relations Committee (SPRC) has the responsibility and opportunity to assist each person in discerning her or his call to ministry. The SPRC can help in discerning the authenticity of a call, and eventually confirming or denying the call by posing questions such as: *Does this person manifest the necessary gifts and grace needed for effective pastoral ministry? Is God calling this person to ministry?* After hearing the response to these questions, the SPRC is sometimes compelled to say *no* to a candidate for ministry.

Perhaps the most critical checkpoint along the path to ordained ministry is the District Committee on Ordained Ministry (DCOM). This Committee has the awesome challenge of attempting to recognize a *diamond in the rough* (i.e., *Does this person demonstrate the necessary skills for effective ministry in The United Methodist Church?*). The DCOM, through the leadership of its chairperson and the district superintendent, must discern the strengths and weaknesses of each person in the candidacy process.

As appropriate, the DCOM may choose to recommend specific steps to strengthen a person's readiness for ministry. For example, a Committee might suggest learning a second language, participating in a short-term mission experience in a country that is culturally different from the candidate's background, or seeking a ministry internship in a congregation of a different culture than the candidate's own. *Is this person cross-culturally competent?* or *Is this person willing to become cross-culturally competent?* The answers to such questions are essentials to successful ministry in cross-racial and cross-cultural situations.

The Conference Board of Ordained Ministry (BOOM) also plays a critical role in preparing pastors for the work of ministry. It is the last checkpoint where persons are recommended for ministerial orders. The Board establishes ordination standards and requirements on behalf of the annual conference in light of the minimum requirements of the *The Book of Discipline of The United Methodist Church 2004*, and accepts persons into ministry according to those standards.

Given their responsibility for the recruitment of clergy, the BOOM, in consultation and cooperation with the Cabinet, has the opportunity to recruit people who meet the above standards, particularly when it comes to cross-cultural competency. Moreover, there is also an opportunity to train persons to become bilingual and bicultural. Fortunately, various resources of the Ministerial Education Fund are available to assist the funding of such a program.

In addition, the BOOM's role is enmeshed in the educational enterprise that prepares people for ministry, namely theological seminaries and training programs that license pastors for ministry. Ideally, the BOOM should maintain a regular dialogue with the seminaries offering feedback and guidance on the type of training that is needed most. For example, each United Methodist seminary faces the challenge of preparing pastors to minister in a multicultural society. This goal can be achieved with a faculty that is not only multicultural, but also cross-culturally competent. Although immersion in a diverse curriculum is critical, students also need opportunities to participate in multicultural field experiences. The various licensing schools for pastoral ministry also bear a similar responsibility.

Ultimately, a person's cultural competence transcends *matters of the head* and becomes a *passion of the heart*. Minority and ethnic-minority pastors in a majority culture need this kind of passion. It follows then that there is also a need for *majority pastors* who have this passion. What would The United Methodist Church be like if all pastors possessed this kind of passion?

The vision and aspiration of all those who engage in the ministry of The United Methodist Church is to labor together with passion and dedication by crossing boundaries and transcending human-made barriers. Such a vision can only be realized when cabinet members to SPRC members acknowledge and affirm that *all* people are needed, if God's holy church is truly to be built.

ACKNOWLEDGMENTS

Effective pastoral ministry always has partners and colleagues. They not only inspire and influence us to succeed in church ministry but they share our pains and joys in our ministerial journey as well.

We could not have written this book without the collaboration of many influencers. It is hard to name all of them as that list includes a number of parishioners, pastors, district superintendents, and bishops.

All three of us are deeply grateful to God for these wonderful people of God without whom we would not have been able to succeed in our church ministries.

We also want to acknowledge the role the staff members of the Abingdon Press played right from the outset of submitting the manuscript, especially to Kathy Armistead, Ph.D., for her unfailing support and constant encouragement through out the production process. Her superb correspondent skill and the fine team of editorial staff enabled us to bring the manuscript to its final shape and concise form.

We also want to acknowledge the never failing support of our spouses and family members. Without their help and patience throughout our ministries, we would not be where we are today!

We sincerely hope this book will enable the churches and pastors in cross-racial and cross-cultural ministries to become more effective agents in serving their God-given communities.

Finally, we dedicate this book to The United Methodist Church for its boundary-transcending commitment to global mission.

Ernest S. Lyght
Glory E. Dharmaraj
Jacob S. Dharmaraj

THE CONTEXT AND PURPOSE OF THIS MANUAL

Although studies on cross-racial and cross-cultural pastoral appointments have been conducted by several United Methodist annual conferences, surveys and research have been performed by a few general agencies of the denomination, and personal interviews and group sessions have been conducted by some individuals and seminarians across the country, *few documents have been prepared and published by those who are actually engaged in cross-racial and cross-cultural pastoral ministry*. Even so, those documents barely scratch the surface of the issues that surround such appointments. In addition, many of these documents are heavy on analysis, yet weak on substance.

Further, a few regional- and national-level meetings have been called to study and address the concerns related to cross-racial and cross-cultural appointments. Attendance at such gatherings has leaned primarily toward people who have noted problems from the *top down*, rather than from the *bottom up*. Many of these people have little if any experience as a minority or an ethnic minority, or as a cultural, racial, or linguistic outsider. Documents based on surveys and interviews alone do not do justice to the concerns and issues surrounding cross-racial and cross-cultural appointments.

Malcolm Browne writes about authentic communication and meaningful representation in *Muddy Boots and Red Socks: A Reporter's Life*. The book features stories of war, romance, and human emotions. In writing about Vietnam Browne says, "There were two kinds of observers. Those who heard about the war from others and those with muddy boots. I preferred the latter."

Whether one talks about the battlefield or church, firsthand experience with muddy boots and soiled hands makes one's communication more authentic and far-reaching. While serving as Episcopal leader of the former Central Illinois Conference, which has a predominantly Anglo membership, Bishop Woodie W. White, an African American, asked the delegates to the Annual Conference in 1991, "You may accept me as your bishop in this conference but will you accept me as your pastor if I were appointed to a local church?" It was a daunting question that still defies a simple answer.

A minority or ethnic-minority pastor appointed to lead a congregation comprised of a different racial or cultural background finds not only a challenging task, but also a witnessing ministry in our modern society. The corporate world has no problem integrating people from many different backgrounds for a common goal. Unfortunately, the church of Jesus Christ lags far behind in this area. The United Methodist Church, however, through its missional commitment and General Conference action, serves as a pioneer and pathfinder in making cross-racial and cross-cultural pastoral appointments.

Many Faces, One Church: A Manual for Cross-Racial and Cross-Cultural Ministry, in contrast to previously published resources on cross-racial and cross-cultural ministry, is written by pastors and a lay mission-practitioner with minority and ethnic-minority experiences in The United Methodist Church. This is the book that *we* wish had been available at the beginning of our pastoral ministries.

Many Faces, One Church:

• was created by pastors and a layperson with scar tissue acquired from their work in the ministry trenches. The guidance and advice presented here comes from those wearing muddy boots and hard-hats, while still engaged in cross-racial and cross-cultural ministry.

• shares a personal story born out of experience to the profound perplexity of current ministerial life in The United Methodist Church. Each of us can bear witness to what we have seen and experienced, and we want to share our stories with others.

• gives voice to numerous unheard pastors and their spouses who have expressed their joys and sorrows concerning cross-racial and cross-cultural ministry. Through our research, we met with caucus groups, pastors, district superintendents, bishops, general agency staff, and laity across the denominations. *Many Faces, One Church* brings together their thoughts, suggestions, and insights that can hopefully lead to more effective cross-racial and cross-cultural appointments and ministry.

During our own decades of ministry in cross-racial and cross-cultural ministries, we have been defeated, yert have succeeded, agonized and rejoiced, wept and laughed, yet we believe that God has called us to this type of ministry.

• attempts to identify the changing dynamics in church and society, and highlight issues that too often serve as barriers between ecclesiastical leaders and minority and ethnic minority pastors. Our hope through the book is to foster dialogue, mutuality, and partnership so that groups and individuals at every level of the church can function as true servants of God.

• empowers pastors from minority and/or ethnic minority communities, and increases their awareness of the challenging ministerial tasks that accompany serving in cross-racial and cross-cultural pastoral appointments.

• is intended for ethnic minority pastors who speak English as a second language, as well as those pastors from other denominations and cultures. The chapters in the pastors section of Part II provide valuable insights and suggestions that can help ethnic minority pastors successfully navigate American culture and minister effectively within United Methodism.

• contains practical suggestions to encourage and help minority and ethnic minority pastors work smarter, overcome fear and prejudices, and be effective pastors. Moreover, *Many Faces, One Church* also strives to map the territory between the church in mainstream culture and pastors from other cultures, while helping both better understand each other.

• provides a friendly reminder to all pastors serving in cross-racial and cross cultural contexts that they are not alone and that others have walked the same road and succeeded.

• strives to create awareness among Anglo clergy and laity that the Body of Jesus Christ is one, which is an essential element everyone must embrace if the Body is to function efficiently. Being different does not mean being inferior, but can, in fact, be a source for enrichment and fulfillment.

Many Faces, One Church is a work-study manual. It offers a framework for energizing laity who work with minority and ethnic minority pastors in the local church setting, and encourages pastors actively engaged in cross-racial and cross-cultural pastoral ministries and those who supervise them. Collectively, they *all* are carving a ministerial path that is both unique and complex.

Our hope is that *Many Faces, One Church* will be used in SPRC meetings, BOM gatherings, cabinet rooms, and seminary and training classrooms to study, discuss, and incorporate eclectic ideas and thoughts that lead to making church ministry more joyous.

Finally, our hope is that the reader will take what he or she learns here and translate it into action that leads the Body of Christ from many to one.

Part I

Why? Cross-Racial and Cross-Cultural Ministry

CHAPTER 1

MINISTRY: A BISHOP'S REFLECTIONS

Ministry is both religious and cultural. The person in ministry answers the call to ministry out of her or his own cultural context and religious experiences. Every person's understanding of God is influenced by one's cultural experiences, or the lack of such experiences beyond one's own cultural context.

Religion is personal and, to some degree, private. Ministry, however, is neither public nor private. Ministry is relational and beckons the person in ministry to cross over cultural boundaries.

The practice of ministry may even lead a person to the places where one's religious beliefs are challenged and transformed, and/or strengthened and renewed. The practice of ministry in a cross-cultural context can yield such a reward for both pastor and parishioner. For me the practice of ministry in several cross-racial, cross-cultural contexts was a transforming experience. It was certainly the same for at least some of the congregations that I served and some of the parishioners with whom I journeyed on the path.

The Journey into Ministry

My personal journey in ministry is both religious and cultural. The journey is a continuing one. My understanding of ministry is evolving and becoming more global in its breadth. I have gained a growing appreciation for what God is doing in the world and in my life. All of these dynamics are factors that enhanced my ministry over time.

The journey began with my parents, who grew up in a racially segregated rural society on the eastern shore of Maryland. The general time frame for them, from birth through high school, was the first twenty-five years of the twentieth century.

My father, William, grew up on a tiny farm outside of Cambridge, while my mother, Attrue, grew up on a small farm near Kingston. Both parents were nurtured in a single-parent extended family. Dad's mother reared him, and Mom's father reared her. Each family actively participated in the nearby Methodist church, where the children learned about God, Jesus Christ, and the Holy Spirit. My parents learned how to cope with a racially segregated society in a positive manner.

William and Attrue met each other while attending Princess Anne Academy in Princess Anne, Maryland. Their Christian formation continued in this Methodist secondary school, which later became a state college. Regular attendance at chapel services was a part of their schedule. Dad paid his tuition costs by saving his money for several years, but later dropped out of school so that he could provide financial support for his mother and other family members. By contrast, Mom's father paid the majority of her tuition costs, although she worked too. The reality is that Dad grew up in poverty and Mom grew up on the edge of poverty.

They went to the Academy because the public schools in their respective communities did not provide schools of excellence for African American students at the secondary level. The public schools were separate and unequal, so my parents turned to the African American church's school for their education. After graduation, Dad continued his education at Morgan College, a Methodist institution at the time, and he completed his theological education at Drew University.

Although my parents grew up in a racially segregated society, at various times they both worked on jobs that placed them in the homes of Anglo employers. In that setting they interacted with Anglo family members. They learned to function in the culture of the African American community, as well as the culture of the majority Anglo community, while enduring the pain of racial segregation.

I was born into a racially segregated society. The walls of separation in this society did not begin to tumble in a significant way until public school desegregation began in 1954. This was the same society that my parents matured in as American-born citizens.

My birth preceded the end of World War II and the beginning of the baby boom generation in 1946 by three years. At the end of the war that brought liberation to several European nations, African Americans who had served in the U.S. Armed Forces returned home to a still-segregated society. The baby boom generation, which spanned from 1946 until the mid sixties, was a time of racial volatility and social change, as well as an epoch of scientific achievement.

The U.S. Supreme Court did not outlaw segregation in the public schools until 1954. The long struggle to demolish the walls of segregation began to climax with the Civil Rights Movement of the 1950s and 1960s. The Montgomery, Alabama Bus Boycott began in 1955. Dr. Martin Luther King Jr. was assassinated in 1968. Today, the struggle continues as The United Methodist Church confronts racism and white privilege within and without.

Racism has both religious and secular characteristics. Racism is at home in the church and in the general society. Racism is deeply embedded in the U.S., and is ensconced in the hearts of numerous men and women.

Education provided the context for the beginning of my transition from a segregated society to an integrated community. Prior to 1955, I attended an all-black elementary school, where there were a few Anglo teachers, in Atlantic City, New Jersey.

When my family moved to Wilmington, Delaware, in the spring of 1955, I enrolled in a newly integrated elementary school. Wilmington had begun to desegregate its public schools because of the 1954 *Brown vs. the Board of Education* U.S. Supreme Court school desegregation decision. From that point on I attended predominantly Anglo public schools. We had always lived in a black neighborhood until we moved to Wilmington, where we lived in an integrated neighborhood.

Growing up in America provided a peculiar bicultural experience that helped shape me as a person. The shaping process began with my parents who conveyed parts of their own cultural heritage that had shaped their lives. I do not remember when I first became aware that America was divided into black and white, and rich and poor. I knew that I was black, but I was taught to know and believe that *I am somebody*. Although we were poor, I did not know it at the time.

My parents did not dwell on skin color, nor did they focus on our economic status. They, with their parental encouragement and strict discipline, taught me and my siblings to strive for excellence in all of life's endeavors. They taught us to be decent human beings and to treat all people with respect. We learned to love all of God's children, regardless of their color. They nurtured us in Methodism by precept and example.

In perhaps subtle ways, I learned that African Americans lived in a certain part of town, usually on the other side of the tracks. I learned that I had to be *careful* when I was in an Anglo neighborhood, but I seldom went there and rarely alone. In essence, I learned that there are two cultures, one black and one white, and that I would have to live in both. This learning was accomplished initially by observing my parents' manner of moving among cultures. In time, I learned my own adaptations as I matured in America.

Exposure to a mixed neighborhood, enrollment in racially integrated schools, and parental influence helped me develop self-assurance and an appreciation for personal excellence. Our immediate neighbors in Wilmington were Italian, thus exposing me to Italian culture and Catholic religious practices. A predominantly Anglo high school faculty guided my learning experiences as a student. While some of these teachers harbored deep racial prejudices, the majority encouraged me to excel in my studies in spite of any personal racial prejudice. It was my parents, though, who affirmed me at all times and encouraged me along the way.

The college years opened my mind, and my world, to a more global perspective. Although Morgan State University was an African American college, it had an integrated faculty and an international student body. I met people from other nations and continents. These experiences broadened my perspective regarding people and cultures.

The seminary years at Drew University, 1965–68, provided a synthesis for my experiences up to that point. I was preparing for fulltime pastoral ministry. During this period, the nation was at war in Vietnam. The Civil Rights Movement was marred by riots across the nation. The racially segregated Delaware Conference of the Methodist Church came to an end in 1965.

In 1966 I applied for a position as a student assistant minister. I was hired to work as the student minister at the Community Methodist Church in Roselle Park, New Jersey, an all-white suburban community. I was well received by the congregation, although there were some parishioners who were a bit reticent about my presence at first. Over time, as we became better acquainted, these reticent persons warmed up to my presence and ministry. One even invited me to his home for a meal. This congregation accepted me as a person learning to do ministry, and they supported me in the process. I gained some firsthand experiences with Anglo culture.

When I began the journey into ministry as a candidate for ordained ministry, I assumed that my ministry would have its genesis and ending in the African American church. My call to ministry was answered in the Delaware Conference, a segregated entity that licensed me as a local pastor, and nurtured me as a youth. The laity and the clergy of the Conference helped me to hear the call. Desegregation and the abolishment of the Central Jurisdiction ignited the demise of the Delaware Conference while I was still in seminary. I wanted the Conference to ordain me, but it was not to be so.

After integration began, the Peninsula Conference ordained me as a Deacon in 1966 and Elder in 1968. When I was ordained as an Elder, my father joined Bishop John Wesley Lord in laying hands on me. In that same session of the Annual Conference, Dad retired. In a real sense he passed the mantle of ministry to me. He had helped me bridge two cultures, African American and Anglo, just as he had learned to bridge two worlds. He also had helped me understand that ministry is both religious and cultural. Ministry is relational.

As I reflect on my journey in ministry, I have learned that it is important to appropriate our life experiences in a positive way as we traverse life's journey. Several observations are apropos here:

- Ministry is both religious and cultural.
- Ministry is relational.
- Ministry is cultural, yet not bound by culture.
- The practice of ministry in a cross-cultural setting can be transforming.

Ministry in the Midst of Diversity

American society is increasingly diverse in terms of race, ethnicity, language, and culture. Moreover, the world is culturally diverse. This diversity is reflected somewhat in The United Methodist Church. The reality is that all we know and do is somehow viewed through the prism of culture. Culture then becomes a mediator, a kind of filter, either positive or negative. It is clear that cultural diversity in the U.S. and in The United Methodist Church is increasing rather than decreasing. Yet one simply has to look around the neighborhood and listen to see and hear diversity. In the postmodern world, the call to ministry occurs in the context of diversity.

Responding to the call to ministry involves multiple choices. First, the matter of answering God's call requires a *yes* or *no* decision. When the answer is *yes*, it is a *yes* to God. It is a *yes* to God's people, who have helped the person called to hear the call. It is a *yes* that expresses one's willingness to serve the entire diversity of God's people, including the poor. That is a gigantic *yes*. That is a *yes* in the Wesleyan spirit.

Second, a *yes* to God's call requires a person to engage in spiritual growth and development and to inform oneself through education. Spiritual preparation is a discipline and a lifetime commitment for people in ministry. A seminary education is a major part of the minister's preparation, which helps broaden one's theological and spiritual horizons. John Wesley believed that the quest for knowledge should be a systematic endeavor, lasting for a lifetime.

Third, when saying *yes* to God's call one has the choice of seeking ordination in The United Methodist Church. Ordination as an Elder in the UMC is linked with membership in an Annual Conference. Such membership, among other things, involves commitment to an episcopal form of church governance.

Ministers participate in an appointive system, as opposed to a call system. Ministers and laity alike, who unite with the UMC, consent to live in covenant with each other based on the rubrics of *The Book of Discipline*. The *Discipline*, of course, contains the covenants by which we agree to live together as United Methodists. The UMC is a denomination committed to racial inclusiveness and open itinerancy in the midst of cultural diversity.

Fourth, all Christians are called to be in ministry, which is to be in relationship with one's sisters and brothers. Some people are called by God to enter into specific forms of ministry—lay ministry, the ministry of a Deacon, the ministry of an Elder, as well as other categories of ministry. Some are called to be pastoral ministers, while others serve in a variety of extension ministries. As disciples of Jesus Christ, we choose to engage in specific ministries, whether we are laity or clergy. A person in ministry must live out her or his call to ministry.

The main focus of this book is pastoral ministry; however, the ideas shared here can be helpful in a variety of ministries and ministerial settings. A useful practice is always to appropriate what we have learned for the practice of our ministry in whatever places it occurs, such as the local church, the military, the hospital setting, or the mission field.

Each person who answers the call to ministry brings a variety of gifts to whatever form of ministry he or she enters. We bring our very being to ministry. We are disciples of Jesus Christ. We are human beings born on planet earth.

Jesus too brought a variety of gifts into his ministry. First, he was a Jew whom Luke described as one who "increased in wisdom and in years, and in divine and human favor" (Luke 2:52). Second, Jesus understood his own Jewish culture, but he was not bound by his culture. He dared to step *outside of the box*. Third, Jesus had a deep appreciation of his own faith tradition, as defined by the Jewish religion, yet he was able to transcend these traditions in order to carry out his ministry. Jesus said, "Do not think that I have come to abolish the law or the prophets; I have come not to abolish but to fulfill" (Matthew 5:17). Fourth, Jesus exhibited to his hearers a wellspring of theological understanding and insight. On one occasion, while still a teenager, Jesus' parents found him in the temple listening to his elders and posing questions to them. "And all who heard him were amazed at his understanding and his answers" (Luke 2:47).

So we bring our ethnicity and race, our culture, our faith tradition, and our theological understanding to the practice of ministry. These are some of our gifts for ministry. One has to realize, however, that these very gifts act as a mediator, which can be a positive or negative screen.

Pastoral Ministry

As we give additional consideration to the ministry of cross-cultural appointments, I want to reflect further on this ministry by reviewing briefly my own pastoral appointments in reverse chronological order. My last pastoral appointment at the historically black St. Mark's UMC lasted ten years (1979–89). My ministry there was informed by an accumulation of experiences in prior parishes. By then I was a much wiser pastor, having learned to employ my God-given gifts for ministry in a more resourceful manner. I learned to be a more effective pastoral leader because I was able to draw from a wellspring of knowledge, wisdom, and practical experiences. The streams flowing from the previous pastoral appointments fed this wellspring.

My third pastoral appointment (1976–79) was at Old Orchards UMC, an all-white suburban congregation in Cherry Hill, New Jersey. There were fewer than six African

American members in the congregation, and we seldom saw other African Americans in the supermarket. I was in a different culture, but it proved to be a rewarding, learning, and growing experience. This congregation introduced me to new forms of creative worship. They taught me to be in dialogue with laity. They compelled me to stretch. I had to broaden my horizons and boundaries. The experience there caused me to carefully examine myself, my leadership style, and the leadership role in which I had been placed.

The second pastoral appointment (1972–77) was the Church of the Good Shepherd in Willingboro, New Jersey. This was a congregation in racial transition, with a mix of about 60 percent Anglo and 40 percent African American. It was a former Evangelical United Brethren congregation, and I was the first Methodist pastor and the first African American pastor. There were a variety of cultural experiences operative in this situation. It was incumbent upon me to relate to the different ethnic and racial groups and their respective cultures. At the same time I was compelled to learn how to hold the expressions of the different cultures in a creative tension. Here are several examples of this creative tension:

- We sang from both the UM hymnal and the Evangelical United Brethren hymnal. In addition, both hymnals were in the pew racks.
- We added gospel music to our hymnody.
- We started a racially integrated gospel choir.
- We wove the various cultural strands together in the worship services.

In June 1968 I was appointed to my first pastoral appointment at St. Mary Street UMC, an African American congregation in Burlington, New Jersey. Two years later I was given additional responsibility for the all white Union UMC in Burlington. I was now pastor of a two church charge in one community—one congregation was African American and the other was Anglo. Unfortunately, I was not given any training to prepare me to assume pastoral responsibility for this cross-cultural, cross-racial appointment during the heat of the Civil Rights struggle. I was compelled to tap the reservoir of my own limited pastoral experience and bicultural understanding of life.

I quickly learned some things about all of God's people:

- Regardless of race, people want to hear the good news preached with integrity and passion.
- People want to be comforted when they are in pain.
- People, when they are feeling lonely, want to know that they have a pastoral friend and confidante.
- People want to know that someone is holding them in prayer, especially in a time of personal crisis.
- People want to know that their pastor loves them.
- People, ultimately, want their pastor to provide effective pastoral leadership.

When we get to know people of a different cultural group or racial group, the barriers that separate us begin to fade away, or at least become less of an obstacle.

Pastoral Leadership

Pastoral leaders need certain universal leadership qualities in addition to the various particular gifts that a person might possess.

1. First and foremost, any pastoral leader needs to possess a genuine and unqualified **love of people**. It is difficult to do effective ministry when the congregation suspects that their pastor does not love them. People know to what extent the pastor does or does not love them, especially the children.
2. Second, a pastor needs to demonstrate **openness** to people, their culture, and their ideas. Openness is characterized often by a willingness to listen to the thoughts, feelings, and opinions of other people.
3. Third, **flexibility** is required in terms of one's leadership style. The pastoral leader must not only be flexible in terms of her or his leadership style, but also be open to the presence of a variety of leadership styles in the congregation. Congregational expectations of their pastoral leader, of course, will vary among different cultural groups. I could not exercise the exact same leadership in each of the ministry settings where I was assigned, because each setting was different.

The assumption in this book is that all congregations want to have an effective pastoral leader. This pastoral leader needs to be a spiritual leader who knows Jesus and who can invite others to join him or her on the pilgrim journey of spiritual growth. Such a spiritual leader eagerly partners with lay spiritual leaders who are also on the path.

Ultimately, *technicolor* is the shade of our ministry, not black and not white. From an historical perspective in America, we have had a tendency to view life only in terms of one color or the other. There are people of many colors in our society, because we live in a cosmopolitan community. The clergy in the UMC is also made up of people of different colors, who represent a variety of cultures, nationalities, and language groups.

Professor Harold J. Recinos contends that we need leadership that is cross-culturally *competent.* As we minister among different racial and ethnic populations, we need to enhance our capacity through cultural education. This enhancement needs to include increased sensitivity and awareness and increased cultural knowledge, which translates into changed behaviors and attitudes. Cultural diversity must be valued. There must be a way of doing cultural self-assessment if the level of cultural competence is to be raised.

Moreover, seminaries and Annual Conferences must assume an active role in preparing pastors to be cross-culturally competent. The individual pastor must also assume responsibility for becoming cross-culturally competent. A part of this task is to gain an understanding of and an appreciation for the many cultures in our world, our nation, and our neighborhoods.

The United Methodist Church is a global community, and it has a global constituency, thus requiring clergy who are culturally competent. One method is for seminaries to regularly provide opportunities for students to encounter other cultures as a part of their theological education. Cultural competency means to engage a culture in terms of its religious, political, economic, historical, economic, and social life. Obviously, a student cannot engage dozens of cultures, but could engage one culture in depth. Such engagement opportunities would raise the level of sensitivity about various cultural concerns.

There are certain fundamental dynamics that are dominant in the practice of effective ministry, regardless of culture:

- Partnership
- Relationships
- Mutuality
- Spiritual Leadership
- Cultural Competence
- Willingness to Learn
- Presence

These dynamics are present in every pastoral ministry situation where there is effective pastoral leadership. This is not an exhaustive list, but it provides the basic ingredients that enable a pastor to lead in a variety of situations. The truth is that no pastor is going to be effective in all situations; yet, effective pastoral leaders tend to be effective in most situations. Perhaps this is true because such persons approach new situations with an open mind and an open heart. They employ and seek to live out the fundamental dynamics outlined above.

Pastors and congregations who enter into cross-racial, cross-cultural ministry must do so with open hearts, open minds, and a determination to learn together and grow together as they open their doors to such a ministry. All pastoral ministries are difficult, and cross-racial, cross-cultural ministries are even more so. These ministries are complex. Such ministries require that the participants, pastor, and congregation be prepared and open to a new way of doing God's work.

Bishop Ernest S. Lyght

CHAPTER 2

CONNECTIONALISM AND CROSS-RACIAL APPOINTMENTS

An immense asset of The United Methodist Church is its connectional system. Through its connectional system, a network of general agencies and a global web of Annual Conferences are engaged in the task of Christian ministry and witness. *The Book of Discipline*, the church's official guide, defines it as:

> Connectionalism in the United Methodist tradition is multi-leveled, global in scope, and local in thrust. Our connectionalism is not merely a linking of one charge conference to another. It is rather a vital web of interactive relationships. We are connected by sharing a common tradition of faith, including our Doctrinal Standards and General Rules; by sharing together a constitutional polity, including a leadership of general superintendency, by sharing a common mission, which we seek to carry out by working together in and through conferences that reflect the inclusive and missional character of our fellowship; by sharing a common ethos that characterizes our distinctive way of doing things.[1]

Connectionalism Is a Culture

Connectionalism creates a culture that builds a basis for ministerial alignment within the denomination. This alignment centers around a core set of Christian beliefs and basic operational principles such as *church and administration, proclamation and worship,* and *mission and evangelism.* This connectional culture grounds pastors and laity in something historic, global, and missional, while nurturing oneness and unity within the denomination. Moreover, it binds all local churches together under an organizational principle, which, in turn, fosters lasting bonds with Methodists everywhere. It is incredibly powerful and unique.

Connectionalism is the tie that keeps United Methodists aligned even as we rush toward a distant horizon. It is also a de facto recruiting, ministering, and equipping tool, which naturally winnows out pastors and behaviors that fail to support the mission and ministry of the denomination. In addition, connectionalism is

- team-oriented and rejects self-servers;
- the Church's spiritual cord and missional tie with a rich heritage that is passed from generation to generation;
- a concept meaning global contact, whose basis is to transcend and convert to the Methodist family. We, in turn, also observe, listen, and learn to let global Methodism influence our local missional commitment.

Consequently, pastors are measured by their team and cooperative skills, since the connectional family and collective witness are more important than individual fiefdoms.

Praxis Connectionalism Is a Mission

Connectionalism also provides a context for mission and evangelism. The context for mission and evangelism is the whole world, which includes the United States. Moreover, the goal of missional context is to lead participants to transformation, acceptance, and mutuality for the cause of Christ's mission. The concept and practice of connectionalism eliminates boundaries while creating mission opportunities.

Our world has become too complex, interdependent, fast moving, and uncertain to predict what will happen in the next few days, weeks, and months—much less years. However, connectionalism has proven its adaptability and flexibility, which offers us confidence that the church will be available to contribute, and to support the needs of our mission partners.

Connectionalism also helps mission engagement triumph and enables local churches to witness in their communities and the world. It enables leaders to think globally while working toward local solutions. By doing so, the denomination is better able to conceptualize the future, identify cross currents, and develop new ways to grow in this dramatic era of change and globalization. We can take this same idea of connectionalism and multiply its effectiveness through cross-racial and cross-cultural appointments. Such appointments enable the church to navigate major global mission trends that significantly impact a congregation's spiritual vitality and daily witness.

Rather than an abstract concept, connectionalism is a mission practice that builds relationships. The world may be a parish to serve and build, but congregations are formed locally, from Boston to Beijing and Buenos Aires to Bombay. In order to maneuver through this maze of volatile uncertainty, the church needs transformational avenues such as partnership not paternalism, integration not isolation. Connectionalism is the opposite of imperialism. Unfortunately, too often it is interpreted only in terms of dollars, rather than in human potential. For example, the voice of the traditionally receiving churches and historically dependent congregations in the global south have been muted and/or silenced since they have nothing to offer materially.

Fear of incorporating economically weak and racially different partners continues to dominate the North American church and mission agenda. After all, incorporating the *other* sometimes creates conflict and embarrassment. However, the practice of true connectionalism removes such fears and faulty notions. The essence or core of connectionalism is the ministry of sharing. Paul wrote in 2 Corinthians 8:13-15, "I do not mean that there should be relief for others and pressure on you, but it is a question of a fair balance between your present abundance and their need, so that their abundance may be your need, in order that there may be a fair balance. As it is written, 'The one who had much did not have too much, / and the one who had little did not have too little.'"

Connectionalism and Pastoral Appointments

Cross-racial and cross-cultural (CR/CC) appointments as practiced presently in The United Methodist Church give a nod of affirmation to the connectional system.

Through CR/CC appointments, the church rises out of the long isolation (and missional triumphalism!) of the global north that believes it can only *send* missionaries, and knows more about people, culture, and religions than others do. This premise says, "We have nothing new to learn from others."

The fact is fellow Christians, especially Methodists from other parts of the world, know more about us than we know about them and their churches. They know our language since they have studied in our colleges and seminaries, and attended our churches and conferences. Moreover, now that they are growing spiritually and numerically faster than those in the global north, it is our turn to learn about mission and ministry from them.

Through cross-racial and cross-cultural appointments, United Methodists:

- broaden their approach to mission by realizing this means both *sending* and *receiving.* God's church is interdependent.
- speak a language that evokes the common bond of Christianity, namely, oneness and unity, and gives credence to the concept of connectionalism. No district or conference that lives in isolation and indifference or contempt for CR/CC appointments can claim to be truly connectional.
- understand and demonstrate that we are in a new global mission era. *Mission is from everywhere to everywhere.* We are senders and receivers, givers and takers, and partners and partakers.

Consequently, cross-racial and cross-cultural appointments are not about charity or racial representation, but are part and parcel of a missional cause, a justice issue, and a connectionalist fulfillment.

Celebrating Connectionalism

We live in a discontinuous world. All forms of change are reshaping our family, economy, society, and religious landscape. Hence, we must not only study change, but also study how change is changing and prepare others for change. Cross-racial and cross-cultural appointments are about changes in pastoral leadership, as well as in pastoral ministry. The quest for divergence often leads to a quest for convergence. Consequently, a new collective viewpoint emerges. We cannot be selective in our emphases. In order to gain a larger picture of the cross-racial and cross-cultural appointment system, laity and pastors must transcend their local and communal context and move to a higher missional and ministerial ground.

In order for the connectional system to become a witnessing and missional activity the church needs to take one more bold step. Partisan treatment of minority and ethnic-minority pastors must be intentionally incorporated into decision-making circles, as well as in the composition of boards, cabinets, and pastoral leadership. This notion of necessary partisan treatment is advocated by Fumitaka Matsuoka, a contemporary theologian who writes, "Unless the objects of signification, women, people of color and other disadvantaged people of North American societies become the primary signifiers ... the tenacity of our accustomed way ... would most likely remain intact."[2]

In order for connectionalism to thrive and succeed, we must begin the educational process from Annual Conference gatherings to local church worship services. Additionally, bishops and district superintendents must promote connectionalism by continual preaching and writing about the joys and jubilations of cross-racial and cross-cultural appointments, and extolling their missional and Christian virtues.

Diversity is not something churches can accommodate, it is something we need to *celebrate*. Small efforts and minor changes will whittle away barriers. Unless we celebrate the presence of members and pastors representing global Christianity within our midst, the changing demographics and ingrained habits of ethnocentrism will continue to divide and polarize our churches and mission engagements.

Dance in a Circle and Celebrate

A *Summertime Song* is a children's story about a young girl's adventure to a birthday party. Lucy, the young girl, studies the alluring invitation. Deciding to go out in the moonlight to the party, Lucy magically becomes a small leaf. A baby bird appears from nowhere driving a taxi modeled from a nest. Lucy climbs aboard and sets off. Along the way, she invites a mouse to ride with her. Soon they are joined by a slow-moving inchworm who declares: "I inch while I sleep, I inch while I wake, I inch until my little feet ache. But I don't care how long I take, I want a piece of BIRTHDAY cake!" The taxi makes one more stop to pick up a tattered china doll who informs Lucy he was lost in the garden several years ago by a bespectacled girl.

After several adventures, Lucy and her companions arrive at the party and discover that the entire garden is also there—minstrel grasshoppers, a horn-blowing butterfly, and a welcoming crow. It is a scene of inclusion and completion.

The party is disturbed by a nasty owl who threatens to eat everyone. The partygoers confess that it is his birthday they are celebrating, and serve him a birthday cake with candles lit. The owl responds, "Tonight I'll eat cake—not bugs. Do you mind?"

By the end of the party, the slow-moving inchworm has turned into a handsome young moth, the baby bird has learned to fly, the mouse has received a generous commission to make a hat, and the owl falls asleep in a flowerpot. Lucy returns home and gives the doll to his long-lost and delighted owner, Lucy's own grandmother.[3]

We too need one magic evening of perfect resolution, where everyone holds hands and dances in a circle. Such is the graceful dance done by cross-racial and cross-cultural appointments.

In Search of Unity

When the St. Mary Street-Union Parish was formed, it brought together an Anglo congregation and an African American congregation. It was a meeting of cultures. In the early days it was merely the sharing of a pastor that held the two congregations together. Later, we began to seek ways in which we might achieve some degree of unity. What could be done to bring the two cultural groups together in a meaningful spirit of cooperation? We soon realized that music was the common ingredient. A choir, which we named The Parish Singers, was formed, and musicians from both congregations shared in its music leadership. Rehearsals were held once a week. The choir members got acquainted as they rehearsed together, fellowshipped together, and performed together.

Notes

1. *The Book of Discipline* (2004), #109.
2. Fumitaka Matsuoka, "Pluralism at Home: Globalization Within North America," *Theological Education* 26 (Spring 1990), Supplement 1, p. 47.
3. Irene Haas, *A Summertime Song* (New York: Margaret K. McElderry Books, 1998).

CHAPTER 3

AFFIRMING CROSS-RACIAL AND CROSS-CULTURAL APPOINTMENTS

Religious and Cultural Foundation

The United Methodist Church supports cross-racial and cross-cultural appointments because:

- The Bible demands it.
- General Conference mandates it.
- It is an equal opportunity employer.
- It is committed to finding and appointing qualified and committed pastors from various backgrounds who are willing to serve effectively in local churches. During the process, the church works hard to avoid discrimination based on race, gender, age, nationality, or handicapping situation.
- It is a connectional church.

The changing nature of the population and transformation of the demography means:

- The United States is a mission site!
- There is a tremendous shortage of clergypersons.
- The white pool of traditional clergy is shrinking.
- The minority population is projected to increase.
- In the next half century, 50 percent of the U.S. population will be from minority communities.

As a result, Americans will be forced to deal with diversity and integration whether they are prepared or not. Unfortunately, the church of Jesus Christ, which has been a pioneer in so many areas, still needs to be a role model, pace-setter, and path-finder in integrating communities.

We no longer live in a unipolar world, as migration and travel have altered the mobility of the global population. Society is heavily influenced by commerce and trade, with an administrative structure that is based on big corporations, stellar earnings, and high profits. Moreover, outsourcing changed the face of business in the 1990s, and shows no sign of slowing. As competition intensifies and pressure increases to cut costs and boost efficiencies, companies often eliminate non-core functions in order to focus on increasing production speed, building customer relationships, and growing business value.

As the business world has done, the church community in the U.S. has embraced the concept of outsourcing, particularly pastors and religious workers serving inner city and rural congregations. The tremendous shortage of native-born pastors means:

- Fewer young men and women are going into ministry.
- The Immigration and Naturalization Service has acknowledged the clergy shortage by creating a special category, the sixth preference, to process clergy applicants from overseas.
- Young people are reluctant to go to rural, smaller, and multi-point congregations. Even when they do go, the attrition rate among young clergy is significantly high in the first six years. Critics say, "No wonder many multi-point congregations are entrusted to foreign-born pastors!"

Communities are becoming multiracial and multicultural. Modern media and technology have opened the floodgates of information to people from other cultures and racial backgrounds. As a church, if cross-racial and cross-cultural appointments are not supported, the notion that a particular race or group who live in one particular geographical location of the world hold a monopoly over the gospel of Jesus Christ is perpetuated. The church's universal mission is to share the message of the gospel with all peoples, all nations, and all cultures—even within the U.S. Cross-racial and cross-cultural appointments foster global ecumenical cooperation and solidarity between the various manifestations of Christ's church all over the world. Christian mission is not monoethnic or monodirectional. It is *from* everywhere *to* everywhere. We are *all* partners in ministry.

Biblical Foundation

North American churches that sent money and missionaries to other parts of the world for the last two centuries now face their own difficulties as their church membership continues to decline. Millions of Anglo Christians have drifted away from the church, leaving the once dominant North America a new mission site. Conversely, the Christian population in other parts of the world has grown significantly in the last fifty years, with more non-Anglo Christians at present than Anglo. The majority of these Christians live in so-called Two Thirds World countries. However, this shift in the Christian population significantly alters the way we are accustomed to engaging in mission. North American churches are now in the position of needing to *receive* Christian missioners from other racial backgrounds and parts of the world.

Jesus reminds us, "Many will come from east and west and will eat with Abraham and Isaac and Jacob in the kingdom of heaven" (Matthew 8:11). From Jesus' birth to the end of his ministry, the gospels relate that he continually received people of other traditions. For example, the Christ Child was manifested to the wise men from the east. Greeks, Syro-Phoenicians, and Samaritans—"those outside of the fold" as well as numerous others—came to Jesus, and he accepted them. By refusing to accept people who are different, or acknowledge Christians of other traditions and the gifts they offer, we contradict the foundation and cornerstone of the Christian faith.

The church of Jesus Christ has always *been* and *is* a gathering place of people of all kinds—people who, just like you and I, were bought by the blood of Jesus Christ to live, receive, and share fellowship within the church. In the first gathering of Christ's church, there were people from "every nation under heaven" (Acts 2:5). All people are children of God and fellow heirs with Jesus Christ (Romans 8) to God's kingdom.

Such a gathering crosses racial, cultural, national, linguistic, and any other human boundary imaginable. As Paul writes, "There is no longer Jew or Greek, there is no longer slave or free, there is no longer male and female; for all of you are one in Christ Jesus" (Galatians 3:28).

Missional Foundation

The *missional appointment*, and its ecclesiastical history, is the software that drives what is called the connectional system of The United Methodist Church. This operating system progresses with steady regularity throughout denominational history, within its boundaries as well as outward to its various connectional partners. Crucial to the success of the missional appointment and its operating system is its synchronization with the commitment and relentlessness of the various role players. The church's mission principles are designed and executed in collaboration with the boundary-less global Christian community, meaning that everyone within the church has an opportunity to engage in mission.

Christian mission has always been global, ecumenical, and inclusive, which provides a long-range view of mission and ministry. It has an eschatological outlook. Consequently, it gives special meaning to what we do right now in the name of Christ. The end product of Christian mission is developing disciples. As a result, the church and its mission should be the last place that entertains bureaucrats or nurtures hostility and separateness of any kind.

The United Methodist Church is not merely a sending mission body. It receives pastors and missionaries from other parts of the world as well. Hence The United Methodist Church is a site of mutuality in mission. Historically, the U.S. branch of United Methodism has been accustomed to sending and providing resources for churches outside of America. However, ecclesiastically and missionally, we are experiencing a major paradigm shift. If, though, as a church, we strive to understand Christian mission as something *from everywhere to everywhere*, and acknowledge that everyone has gifts to share, our discomfort toward now being receivers of messengers from *outside* will lessen.

Cross-racial and cross-cultural appointments are an opportunity for us to understand and apply the missional concept of *receiving*. In this case, accepting messengers of the gospel from other racial and cultural backgrounds to serve as pastors in local churches is an act of receiving. Moreover, CR/CC appointments are a mission task and a prophetic challenge. Pastors in these settings challenge our traditional ways of doing worship and mission. For example:

- When the gospel is shared by a pastor from another culture with a different approach it is a **hermeneutical challenge**.
- Cross-racial and cross-cultural pastors, through their engagement in local churches and involvement in these communities, transform people inside and outside of the church by their very presence. Hence, CR/CC appointments are a **communal challenge**.

- Too often we are so concerned about preaching to others that we miss hearing God's message from our partners in mission who are from different backgrounds. Hence cross-racial and cross-cultural appointments are a **denominational challenge**.
- Cross-racial and cross-cultural appointments strike at the heart of traditionalism in the local church and uncap the spiritual and missional reserves of new immigrants. Pastors from other cultures interpret the gospel in a new way so that Jesus Christ comes alive in a different way, making cross-racial and cross-cultural appointments an **incarnational challenge**.
- Pastors from outside the U.S. bring a different perspective to Christian values and missional outreach since many have lived as religious minorities in their birth countries. They can readily share new ways of ministering to people who live in our communities. Some of these pastors are the direct or indirect result of Western mission agencies' efforts to make disciples throughout the world. CR/CC appointments are also a **mutuality-in-mission challenge**.

Therefore, leaders of the church must transcend their traditional agenda and begin preaching and writing more about the importance of cross-racial and cross-cultural appointments, and extolling their missional value through connectional practices. By doing so, they and we become part-takers of modern-day mission.

Ecclesiastical Foundation and Its Challenges

Every generation believes that the inventions they discover will revolutionize the world. As humanity progressed from the wheel to steam engines to silicon chips to satellite technology, each generation relied on change, believing in perfection. Still perfection has proved elusive and distant. The same is also true of the church, which constantly mends itself while moving toward perfection as the bride of Christ. The church is *reformata semper reformanda* (i.e., reformed and is always reforming).

United Methodism continually transforms itself. The more profound the church's commitment to connectionalism and participation in global mission, the stronger its desire and longing to become an authentic global church. Absolute integration has yet to be realized within the church, and it may not occur in our lifetime. Regardless of when integration is realized, most important is the effort and the contribution we make along the way. The fact that some cross-racial and cross-cultural appointments have failed to function well does not mean that we need to abandon doing our best to do what is right. The church is still a work in progress. No appointment is, or will ever be, perfect since people are different and will always disagree.

The formidable and visible challenge that cross-racial and cross-cultural appointments present means that bishops and their cabinets must staunchly believe in equality and diversity, and the accompanying disappointments sometimes, *or* move from open itineracy to a congregational call system.

However, everyone must begin to realize that cross-racial and cross-cultural appointments are one more small, but meaningful step toward a true fellowship of all believers who make up the Body of Christ.

Border-Crossing and Boundary-Setting Mission

The topography of the contemporary ecclesiastical construction site is a featureless and weed-ridden terrain. If it is to become a fine habitat for believers, we must create a contour and draw boundaries that help develop the terrain, structure it, and orient ourselves within it. Moreover, contour and boundaries help us focus our attention on a limited piece of property. As we become intuitively and intimately familiar with the terrain or the landscape, we can transcend the boundaries we created and cross the borders to enlarge our terrain. The cycle of creating and transcending boundaries again and again is the circle of life. In fact, it is the paradigm of life both personally and missionally.

Unfortunately, the tendency to value certain people over others is endemic to human nature and most cultures. The church, by virtue of its call to unity and commitment to equality, constantly strives to create and foster an environment that values people of every background. For the church of Jesus Christ in obedience to its missional mandate serves as a brick-maker, construction worker, and bridge-builder—just as its founder is a Master Carpenter.

We as members of the Body of Christ should not lament the rapid changes that take place around us constantly, but rather recognize that we cannot go back in time or wait for the good old days to return. Instead, we need to break the shackles of the past and embrace newness, openness, and innovation by reconceiving current ministries in ways that generate care for the people.

Unfortunately, too many congregations and several spiritual leaders still glorify the traditions and lifestyles of the past. They reminiscence about a Norman Rockwell illustration of early twentieth-century America complete with pristine churches, cozy frame houses, small communities, and thriving main streets. We have yet to learn to let the dead bury the dead (Matthew 8:22), and move forward with the past as an enabler, an abiding past, if you will.

In order to move forward, we need to bury the past, take risks, and cross metaphorical boundaries and physical borders. One of the saddest episodes of Hebrew history is the Israelites wandering in the wilderness for forty years. The weary and worn-out Israelites carried around the 430-year-old bones of Joseph for forty years because they were waiting to bury them in the promised land. What a long journey, and what a weary wait!

The United Methodist Church's Mission Foundation

The United Methodist Church, remaining true to its tradition, is again a pioneer by engaging in the border-crossing mission of making cross-racial and cross-cultural appointments in local churches. Through legislation and other means, the church has become agile and responsible, and created an environment where all pastors and laity can feel welcome and be engaged in ministry.

The future we envisioned concerning CC/CR appointments at the 1996 General Conference has already arrived, and more rapidly than we anticipated. This is due in part to the number of bishops and district superintendents who are open and mission-minded. Moreover, immigration, the change in society, and the greater influx of multiracial pastors on seminary campuses have also been key elements of this change.

Many pastors serving in cross-racial and cross-cultural appointments are encouraged by the General Conference's continued affirmation and Annual Conferences' compliance in making such appointments despite setbacks and challenges. One thing that gives even more hope to these pastors is the way that bishops, district superintendents, Board of Ordained Ministry members, local congregations, and theological institutions are coming together in consensus about the direction and ministry of the denomination in the twenty-first century.

Unfortunately, in some conferences, appointments are driven by reaction and fear. However, in other places, they are fueled by hope. Truly this is a hopeful time, which is good for the denomination and local congregations. Visible signs of integration are evident in many places, which is indeed heart-warming. The UMC is a different church than it was a quarter century ago. Our ministerial method has quietly, but substantially been reshaped to capitalize on the changing dynamics and leadership opportunities within the church.

Seized by an intensity and unity within the Body of Christ, the UMC is poised for the next level that extends the ministerial boundaries of the denomination to the periphery of the world community. However, despite the strides we have made as a denomination, it is still legitimate to ask at this crucial juncture, "Are we indeed capable of more?" The answer is a resounding, "yes."

The Solution Is Integration

If we are to succeed in CR/CC ministry, we will need to work together for each other's success. If we are to solve the thorniest and most widespread problems in our church and community, we must innovate in ways that truly matter. We can begin by taking missional responsibility for all of our actions—with pastors, churches, and laity.

We must be flexible to succeed in ministry. Pastors and churches need to constantly reinvent themselves in order to make the Gospel relevant. We must sustain the best of the past and abandon what is no longer relevant. We have to connect to the people who matter and interpret the message in a way that matters.

Through cross-racial and cross-cultural appointments, the UMC strives to promote an awareness of the global nature of the denomination. Such an act creates an equitable situation for pastors and members to trust each other as mutual members of the Body of Christ, allowing them to minister with each other at the altar of collaboration and partnership. Churches, like other institutions, are works in progress. Only through dynamic commitment to moving ahead can an organization remain successful and faithful.

A great deal has already been achieved, but much remains to be done to realize the immense potential of this church. This will always be true. When the current challenges have been met, new issues, challenges, opportunities, and problems will surface. Some problems will be legitimate, while others will be the result of human frailty. As people come to understand the broader definition of the mission and ministry of Christ's holy church and its challenges, our current problems will dissipate.

The denomination's dynamic commitment to change and its passion to be faithful to God's mission ensures that it will strive to continually meet the needs of congregations and provide multifarious opportunities to fulfill the mission of the church. We need to be persistent and adaptable, committed and focused, and open and vulnerable. After all, we, as a church, are in the early stages of this new missional development. Let's keep our seat belts buckled!

A Taste of New Culture Is Refreshing

My first taste of Korean American culture occurred when I became the pastor of Old Orchards UMC in Cherry Hill, New Jersey. The Old Orchards congregation was housed in a sanctuary that was located adjacent to the Conference Headquarters of the former Southern New Jersey Annual Conference. The Conference building provided shared worship/education space for the Korean United Methodist congregation and shared worship/education/administrative space for the Old Orchards congregation.

It was a profound joy for me to have the opportunity as a pastoral leader to cooperate in various ways with the Korean United Methodist Church congregation. It was a delight sharing with the pastor. On several occasions he invited me to preach for his congregation. He would serve as the translator for my sermons. I have fond memories of sitting at the table with members of the congregation for fellowship and food. It was during those years that I developed a taste for Korean foods and an appreciation for food that was very different from my own cultural menus.

Moreover, I began to learn about Korean culture. As a result I gained a deeper understanding of what it means to be Korean in the U.S. I am still learning and becoming more culturally competent as a result.

(ESL)

CHAPTER 4

MUTUALITY AND MINISTERIAL APPOINTMENTS

As with modern society, the church's mission is constantly moving, changing, and interconnecting. It has a sense of uncertainty and relativity. Some church leaders fear not being "in control" and therefore create their own meaning and interpretation of the church's mission and ministry.

In this non-linear, circular, and ever-moving missional context, one of the best ways the church can attempt to engage in mission today is through the spirit of mutuality and creative opportunities. Mutuality is a missional concept that conveys that we are all in the cause of Christ together. It means having a loving heart, an open mind, and a searching soul filled with the truth of the gospel since we are called to serve one another and bear each other's burden in God's kingdom.

The Bible describes God's kingdom as an inclusive kingdom. "For in Christ Jesus you are all children of God through faith" (Galatians 3:26). Revelation 7:9 describes it: "After this I looked, and there was a great multitude that no one could count, from every nation, from all tribes and peoples and languages, standing before the throne and before the Lamb, robed in white, with palm branches in their hands."

Mutuality and Commitment: A Theoretical Explanation

- Mutuality allows the power of imagination to run free, the moving of the Spirit to operate unfettered, the power of the Resurrection to do miracles.
- Mutuality never ceases to educate, redefine, and update the nature of relationship between partners. It is the moving target of relationships.
- Mutuality in Christian mission is committed to a culture of equality. The partners are bound together for a common cause in order to bring people back to God.
- Mutuality enables the partners to communicate honestly and behave with integrity. They see the world from the other partner's perspective and share the partner's mental map for the future.
- Mutuality demands total trust and absolute transparency. Consequently, it brings partners to engage themselves in straight talk and pure transparency in order to foster a win-win situation.
- There is an intense commitment and confidence on the part of the partners as we practice mutuality in mission, as each one has something to offer to the ministry.
- Shared vision and common purpose motivate and sustain the partners who are engaged in mission and encourage the partners involved to embody God's caring and compassionate love.

- Mutuality is a process of give and take. Making exchanges is the fundamental principle that operates this machinery.
- When the partners who are engaged in this process see something of value that they receive in return, they cooperate and function efficiently.
- Mutuality demands partners to rise above regionalism, parochialism, and all forms of discrimination.
- Mutuality becomes effective when partners acknowledge that their understanding of mission and ministry is partial and limited, and they need others to become wholesome and complete.
- Mutuality becomes witnessing when they are willing to yoke with the weaker or stronger partner because the Bible commands the followers of Christ to maintain unity.
- Mutuality opens a dialogue. The emphasis is on authentic conversation between partners to arrive at a unanimous or a mutually agreeable consensus. It respects differences and works to identify underlying and unstated assumptions. It does not compel consent. It seeks breadth and diversity, rather than focusing on a single context or location.
- Mutuality has a back and forth, receiving and sending movement. In the final analysis, refusal to acknowledge mutuality in Christian mission is to destroy a resource, to annihilate the streams of ministry, to abandon the fountain of life, and to forsake the essence of our faith.
- Mutuality not only takes us back to one common cause to be engaged in mission, but also to the ever-expanding, concentric circles of newly established Christian fellowship.
- Mutuality and oneness of the believers alone can make the church visible in a world of hate and exploitation, oppression and racism, division and selfishness, and can, like John the Baptist, pave the way for the epiphany of Christ.

Mission and Mutuality

When Glory and I flew into Madras, India on a summer morning on British Airlines Flight 292, a few seconds after the landing the flight attendant announced in impeccable English: "Ladies and gentlemen, we are just landing in Madras. Those of you who are coming to India for the first time, have an enjoyable time. Those of you who are returning after several years, WELCOME HOME."

Our landing in India after many years brought sweet reminders of the way I lived as a young man in that part of the world. I would never have guessed then that one day I would be privileged with sharing the gospel in another part of the world, with people of another race, culture, and language . . . and then come home to be welcomed by a British flight attendant.

Instinctively, I grabbed Glory's hand. Drawing an analogy to Christian mission I said, "This is what Christian mission is all about. Look at the way an intercontinental itinerant is welcoming the natives; a British flight attendant receiving the Indian nationals and welcoming them on behalf of their homeland."

Overseas airline attendants leading indigenous travelers to their waiting families reminds me of the way cross-cultural missionaries, foreign-born evangelists, ever-moving circuit riders, and itinerant Bible women led local people to Christ. Is this what *mission in mutuality* is about?

I admire the way flight attendants who work for shuttle airlines between big cities welcome passengers on behalf of the city in which the plane lands. Since Christian ministry is a pilgrim ministry, we are commanded to guide people to Christ and serve God's children in God's name. We are mandated to welcome God's children on behalf of God's kingdom wherever we are sent to minister.

(JSD)

Part II

Who?
The Players and Their Roles

CHAPTER 5

UNDERSTANDING MINORITY AND ETHNIC-MINORITY PASTORS

(For Cabinet, BOOM, and SPRC Members)

Pastors in cross-racial and cross-cultural appointments are not merely servants of the gospel, but also people—human beings—with histories, cultures, emotions, and feelings. Love and concern for others is not an option, but the fundamental tenet of the Christian faith. Love that reaps only advantages and benefits from others, but will not share and also bear another's burdens is illusionary, not Christian.

When churches served by Anglo pastors fail in their missional goals, blame is often placed on the changing demographics or configuration of the community or culture. However, when churches served by minority or ethnic-minority pastors fail, they tend to bear the blame individually. Unfortunately, we live in a world where people are either privileged or exploited on the basis of their social standing. An individual belonging to a dominant social or racial group enjoys not only privilege, but also the luxury of seeing oneself as an individual. For example, a white person is seldom defined by his or her whiteness. A successful white person is simply acknowledged as a highly successful individual, and if he or she fails, the blame is attributed only to that specific individual.

On the other hand, an individual belonging to a subordinate social or racial group is evaluated quite differently. This individual's success is seen as atypical or exceptional, and her or his failure is viewed as symptomatic of the limitations of an entire group. Often minorities and ethnic minorities are seen as a group rather than as individuals.[1]

Crossing Bridges with Caution

Increasingly, minority and ethnic-minority clergy and their families are the recipients of the denomination's efforts to fulfill its commitment to an open itinerant system through cross-racial and cross-cultural appointments. These efforts reflect positively on the church's mission and ministry to and with all people. However, care must be exercised to assure the readiness of congregations, pastoral teams, and clergy families for these appointments.

Overall, minority and ethnic-minority clergy and their families feel that the denomination is moving slowly in its recognition of their presence, their needs, and their desires for "walking in balance" in relation to God, themselves, their families, their ministry settings, the church, and all things. Much is yet to be done in response to their needs.[2]

The church must understand that minority and ethnic-minority pastors operate differently from Anglo pastors, and need to be managed or supervised accordingly. The standard management techniques are not always appropriate since races and genders often operate and socialize differently. Listed below are several key areas where leaders should focus their attention in working with minority pastors:

- Leaders must bear in mind that one size does not fit all when working with minority and ethnic-minority pastors.
- Although minority and ethnic-minority pastors may have cross-cultural experience, they may lack multicultural management skills. When beginning a new appointment, they often assume that pastoral competence is more important than administrative skills. However, they quickly learn that racial prejudice and discrimination can derail their day-to-day administration and ministry.
- Members of congregations and the Cabinet often value the continuity of a local church's ministry. Often their preference is to maintain the status quo of the ministry within the local church and the community's traditional setting. Conversely, minority, particularly ethnic-minority pastors, prefer uniqueness and distinctiveness in ministry. These pastors frequently talk of the larger Body of Christ and promote a global understanding of mission and ministry. Such differences in missional and ministerial focus typically create tension and foster alienation. The district superintendent and Board of Ordained Ministry, however, can assist in such situations by helping find a middle ground that combines uniqueness with continuity.
- Minority and ethnic-minority pastors often feel a deep-seated discomfort and tension concerning the issues that arise in cross-racial or cross-cultural appointments. Many, though, find it difficult to express this discomfort in words. When listening to minority and ethnic-minority pastors, avoid ignoring their concerns simply because they are fumbling for words.
- Understand, trust, and respect the minority and ethnic-minority pastor by maintaining regular contact throughout the year. A district superintendent cannot afford to be a remote figure in cross-racial and cross-cultural ministry.
- Often minority pastors are excluded from social activities not only by their white peers, but also by their own parishioners. One minority pastor shared, "It is terrible to be invited to a ministers' meeting and be greeted by the four ministers that know you, while the other twenty blatantly ignore you, even during the common meal."[3] After an appointment is made the process of integrating the new pastor into the congregation and the ministerial community should begin immediately.

Creating an environment where minority and ethnic-minority pastors feel affirmed and validated falls initially to the Cabinet and BOOM, and continues to members of the Annual Conference, SPRC, and local church boards and members.

Let 'Em In

Minority and ethnic-minority pastors experience again and again the need to prove their pastoral worthiness to the denomination's and local church's leadership. However, solidarity and affirmation from their colleagues and leaders goes a long way in helping them minister effectively. Below are several ideas for supporting and nurturing minority and ethnic-minority pastors:

- The BOOM and Cabinet must be aware of cultural, linguistic, and behavioral consequences when making pastoral appointments.
- In times of crisis, superintendents, in particular, should avoid using patronizing or condescending language. Instead phrases such as "with your knowledge and strengths..." "with God-given skills, you..." are professionally affirming and spiritually enriching.
- Although ethnic pastors may speak with an accent, many read and speak English fluently since they have studied it as a second language since high school.
- District Superintendents should strive to be colleagues and friends, not merely supervisors to minority and ethnic-minority pastors. Pearl S. Buck wrote:

  By birth and ancestry I am an American; by choice and belief I am a Christian; but by the year of my life, by sympathy and feeling, I am Chinese. As a Chinese I say to you what many Chinese have said to me: "Come to us no more in arrogance of spirit. Come to us as brothers and fellow men. Let us see in you how your religion works. Preach to us no more, but share with us that better and more abundant life which your Christ lived. Give us your best, or nothing."[4]

- The district superintendent must stand up for what he or she truly believes. When a minority or ethnic-minority pastor is under attack, the district superintendent must lead by example by shouldering a portion of the criticism. Do not betray minority pastors by saying, "they are new" or "they are not Americanized yet..." and so on.
- When taking minority and ethnic-minority pastors to local churches, the District Superintendent should ask the SPRC to define the missional goals of the church. Write them down, and place the pastor within this context. Note that if there is no clearly defined missional and ministerial expectation, minority and ethnic-minority pastors will quickly be lost.
- Work closely with minority and ethnic-minority pastors. By doing so, all partners involved can define and visualize what successful ministry will look like.

In times of trouble, minority and ethnic-minority pastors, like all pastors, want their peers and supervisors to demonstrate Christian missional solidarity with them. Solidarity in mission action means a praxis of mutuality between the privileged and those denied privilege. In the secular world, people exercise power and authority competitively and adversarially while aiming for mastery or control. In the church, however, community power and authority are characterized by mutuality and partnership rather than sovereignty and supremacy.

District Superintendents have institutional power and authority, status and respect. This power is further augmented by the race, gender, class to which the individual belongs. As a result, it is imperative that they are clear about the power and authority they desire, or that is thrust upon them. Moreover, they must know how to use their power and authority as a "bridge" that connects pastors, rather than one that hangs above their colleagues.

"Authority over" relates to our behaviors, attitude, performance, and evaluation. "Authority with" models for minority and ethnic-minority pastors and others the way to gain authority and respect, if not institutional power, then the power of the Spirit and a knowledge of ministry that the denomination credentials.

Notes

1. See Maurianne Adams, Lee Anne Bell, and Pat Grffin (editors), *Teaching for Diversity and Social Justice* (New York: Routledge, 1997), p. 9.
2. Anne Streaty Wimberley, *One Household, One Hope* (Division of Ordained Ministry, Board of Higher Education and Ministry, 1988), p. 92.
3. *One Household*, p. 69.
4. Quoted by Ray Freeman Jenney, *Speaking Boldly: Essay-Sermons* (New York: Revell, 1935), p. 126.

CHAPTER 6

RECOMMENDATIONS TO THE CABINET, BOARD OF ORDAINED MINISTRY, AND STAFF-PARISH RELATIONS COMMITTEE

For decades, the trend on academic campuses across the country has been specialization—*focused study*. However, the boundaries of specialization are blurring. Hence pastors must become generalists. They need an integrated educational experience. Scientific, technological, and even commercial centers talk about convergence of disciplinary forces, new discoveries, and new ways to reach people and markets. When these converging units grow and expand, often they overlap. By doing so, they inform each other, yielding yet greater results. Seminary education requires the same multidisciplinary and interdisciplinary approach, along with the use of contemporary mission tools.

Unfortunately, few resources are available on integrated subjects. However, pastors still need to be prepared for a new style of ministry. School and other learning institutions need to invest sufficient resources into getting and staying ahead of the curve in this new era. Too often seminaries operate on the principle as if to say, "Here are all the theologies and mission principles that are available. You figure out how to apply them." The result is a mismatched education of what the seminarians have been taught and what they actually need to know to succeed in the local church ministry. Real-world experience is essential. A master's degree in divinity alone will not ensure that a pastor will succeed. If difficulty arises during an appointment, an academic degree carries little weight.

Too often seminaries are far behind the curve when it comes to cross racial and cross-cultural ministry. The task of teaching this area of ministry has been relegated to missionary training institutes. The assumption then is that all pastors will serve in monoethnic communities or the larger mission sites of the world. Since this is no longer the case, we need specific guidelines for curriculum reform that emphasize church growth through cross-racial and cross-cultural appointments, and highlight theories or scientific ways of doing ministry in a changing pluralistic society.

There is also the widespread assumption that a seminary education will enhance a seminarian's ministerial career. Unfortunately, some candidates rely solely on academic degrees to prepare them for pastoral ministry. However, a mentoring/nurturing program could help them recognize that there is little-to-no correlation between theological education and effectiveness in ministry.

Education, experience, willingness, and *dedication*—all have value, but only those who are culturally prepared and able to contextualize their academic learning are prepared to lead a congregation to the next level. This chapter offers suggestions to Cabinet, BOOM, and SPRC members as enhancements for ministries in the local church.

Resourcing

In order for pastors serving in cross-racial and cross-cultural contexts to be effective in their ministry, they must be given adequate and appropriate resources. Church leaders and administrators must trust the abilities of these pastors and their commitment to ministry, and not focus solely on achieving denominational goals. Effective pastoral ministry has to be developed, not simply preserved. This means creating work environments where minority and ethnic-minority pastors can collaborate creatively and effectively.

Pastors must be constantly refreshed and renewed. Each conference, therefore, needs to reinvent its knowledge base periodically. This means selecting and placing a few gifted and talented minority and ethnic-minority pastors in visible, thriving, and growing churches.

In order for cross-racial and cross-cultural appointments to succeed, Cabinet members must manage pastors who are proficient with multiracial, multicultural, and multilinguistic issues and ministry, not just financial or statistical data about local churches and their mundane concerns.

On the other hand, minority and ethnic-minority pastors should be encouraged to take courses in management and organizational skills as part of their continuing education. Such courses could be introduced at the School for License to Pastoral Ministry as well. These courses could be attended soon after or immediately prior to an appointment to a local church. For the most part, seminary courses on church administration are abstract and too unfocused for pastoral candidates born and raised outside of the U.S.

Moreover, it is also a good idea for the members of the Cabinet and BOOM to take courses on multiculturalism and management. As the "gate keepers" into pastoral ministry, the members of BOOM should be trained in how to interview and assess the pastoral worthiness of minority and ethnic-minority candidates. Reading books on cross-racial and cross-cultural communications as a means of understanding people who are different from mainstream Americans is not enough. This is similar to claiming one can understand Indian art after reading one book on Indian paintings. Church leaders can only truly get to know pastors from other backgrounds by personally engaging them and interacting with them.

Another idea is to assign a person from each ethnic community to serve as a liaison (not merely as a CCOM or DCOM member) between the pastor and the Cabinet or the district superintendent. Developing a mentoring or sponsoring program, similar to ombudsmen, that crosses racial and cultural barriers will alleviate many fears and frustrations. Although the Commission on Race and Religion works to address the problems that minorities and ethnic minorities encounter, the Commission functions more as a remote committee than as an intervening or interceding agency.

At least twice a year, district superintendents could provide details on the status of minority and ethnic-minority pastors and their churches. If they are growing, find out why. If they are not growing, what can the Cabinet, district superintendents, and others do to assist them? Such interest would illustrate commitment and generate confidence for pastors and leaders.

Listed below are recommendations from a study conducted by the General Board of Higher Education:

1. The district superintendent should be a "pastor of pastors." Everyone needs someone with whom they can talk, in whom they can confide, and from whom they can receive affirmation. There is need for district superintendents to be sensitive to the politics of race, and be more responsive and understanding of the special needs of ethnic-minority clergy. On issues of appointment, care should be taken to spend time with both the pastor and the spouse. In cases of anxiety and struggle, the DS should actively gain knowledge of and be supportive in nonpunitive ways. The training of the DS should include skills in enabling support systems among ethnic-minority clergy and their families.

2. The conference should provide counseling options and financial assistance for counseling. There should be options for marital counseling and other kinds of counseling. However, care should be taken that counseling is afforded in ways that respect privacy of the clergy and clergy family. A list of ethnic and culturally sensitive counselors is also an important resource to develop.

3. The SPRC needs training to be more sensitive to the supportive needs of clergy and their families. Workshops for SPRC need to be developed at the district and conference level regarding support systems for the concerns of clergy and their families.

4. The Cabinet needs to be as sensitive to the family concerns of clergy as to concerns for the survival of the connectional system.

5. There is need to find salary support for many ethnic-minority clergy that goes beyond the minimum "equitable salary" standards. Many ethnic-minority clergy feel that they are doomed to minimum salary appointments.

6. There is need to work on opening up itineracy and movement across conference lines

7. A cross-racial appointment facilitating committee should be organized at the conference level to assist congregations, pastoral teams, and clergy families in preparation for a positive movement into cross-racial appointments. Such committees would serve as resources in preparatory meetings to the appointment and would provide follow-up resources as needed. A support group of pastors and families in cross-racial appointments might also be organized under the auspices of this committee. Conference sponsorship of the committee may come through the Conference Board of Ordained Ministry.[1]

Through its legislation, the General Conference not only tries to attract and retain minority and ethnic-minority pastors, but also strives to provide an encouraging environment for their creative ministry within the denomination.

As church leaders and administrators move from training session to workshop, and legislation to incorporation, they may be setting a convoluted course toward ministerial success, while ignoring the underlying purpose of cross-racial and cross-cultural appointments. Yet, the voice of minority and ethnic-minority pastors expresses a view different from widely held assumptions, like the cozy but dubious notion that legislation alone will bring changes in the appointment processes and effective ministry in local congregations. Only the coordinated and committed efforts of everyone involved can truly make this a reality.

Notes

1. *One Household,* pp. 111-13.

CHAPTER 7

ANATOMY OF CROSS-RACIAL AND CROSS-CULTURAL APPOINTMENTS

(For Cabinet, Board of Ministry Committees, Staff-Parish Relations Committees)

Concerns over cross-racial and cross-cultural appointments are smoldering across the denomination. Yet few leaders appear to address these concerns openly from the floor of Annual Conferences, district meetings, or local church gatherings. A number of minority and ethnic-minority pastors too often lack adequate training and guidance for successful local church ministry. As a result, they feel left behind with little support to succeed in ministry.

The core of the problem runs deeper than understanding a culture, mastering a language, or knowing the people. It is deeper than preaching and administration. The core of the problem is *change, difference, newness,* and *unpreparedness.* If cross-racial and cross-cultural appointments are to succeed, there must be a change of hearts and minds. There must be a renewed commitment to ministry and the church. There must be willingness to learn, and an openness to receive.

The changes and renewal that are needed demand a new kind of approach, a *missional* approach. Unless cross-racial and cross-cultural appointments are approached from a missional perspective, the entire process will crumble.

Clarification of Mission Reason

Mission does not mean charity work, but rather a priority task. Although charity is a component of the missional structure, the goal is to enhance the purpose of mission work from the *pew* to the *pulpit* to the *public.* Therefore, cross-racial and cross-cultural appointments must be considered a missional issue, not merely a denominational mandate. "We succeed when you succeed," could become the mission statement for this emphasis, and appointments made under the broad concepts of *connectionalism, ecumenicity,* and *partnership* as missional principles.

The goal here is not to advocate for the appointment of more minority or ethnic-minority pastors, who are then supervised more closely. Such advocacy is based on control and power. Rather, a missional approach to such appointments is needed. For mission implies partnership, mutuality, respect, and a willingness to listen, learn, and work with others. In addition, the meaning of cross-cultural and cross-racial appointments needs to be clarified, and the myths and misunderstandings that surround them dispelled. One common misperception concerning cross-racial and cross-cultural appointments is that it is simply another term for quotas or an affirmative action plan. Conversely, a missional atmosphere creates an environment with a level playing field on which all pastors have an opportunity to become effective and succeed.

When we intentionally strive to make cross-racial and cross-cultural appointments more effective as a missional prerogative, barriers are dismantled and an environment for total inclusiveness is created. Such an environment means that everyone plays in the game and winning is guaranteed.

Suggestions for Mission Action

In times of crisis the Cabinet, BOOM, and SPRC members need to stand with unyielding integrity for the cause of mission. These groups must strive to retain, assess, develop, and motivate minority and ethnic-minority pastors. As a means of role reversal and understanding the *minority* experience, Anglo pastors and church members should consider attending minority meetings, fellowships, workshops, or conferences. This would allow them to feel the *invisibility* that minority and ethnic-minority pastors too often feel within the church. In addition, educating members of the conference and advocating the missional principle behind cross-racial and cross-cultural appointments are vital for the success of these appointments. After all, minority and ethnic-minority pastors are a key part of the denomination, not a side attraction. The following are other ideas for mission action:

- Involve everyone in the education process, from local church pastors to leaders of laity at the district and conference level.
- Encourage interaction with and appreciation for the global Christian community, remembering that Christian mission is always global, ecumenical, and communal.
- Create the vision of a global and connectional church, then act with a boundless mentality.
- Speak and write frequently of the conference's and denomination's commitment to global mission.
- Create an environment of trust and love.
- Take a proactive approach to encouraging and making cross-racial and cross-cultural appointments.
- Clarify and interpret the appointment plan.
- Talk and write about the importance of cross-racial and cross-cultural appointments in district and conference newsletters. This is especially necessary for bishops, district superintendents, and BOOM members. If members of conferences and churches are continually informed about such appointments, cynicism, distrust, and noncooperation will begin to fade.

- Distribute press releases that focus on and celebrate the multicultural and multiracial presence within the conference, district, and local congregations.
- Offer an annual education awareness session for pastors, lay leaders, and SPRC to help alleviate potential problems.
- Recognize and openly acknowledge the potentialities of minority and ethnic-minority pastors. Present them in a positive light, showing the church and community the benefit of mutual cooperation.
- BOOM and Cabinet can develop effective guidelines and written tools for each district or conference, such as a requirement for all pastors to have a course on multicultural management and working with diversity. Such guidelines can also be mandated by the School for License for Pastoral Ministry, or as a requirement in the seminary, Course of Study School, or at the School for Continuing Education.
- Hold yearly meetings with minority and ethnic-minority pastors where joys and concerns are shared before beginning the conference appointment process. Meetings convened by the Commission on Religion and Race or other such groups have often become monodirectional and strictly information-gathering sessions. However, a shared acknowledgment that both parties are in ministry together and the failure of one entails the failure of the other will yield lasting results. Hence each group needs to bring to the table their skills and resources that are fundamentally essential for an effective ministry without losing one's identity.

The Gospel Paradox

Shirley Nelson's *Last Year of the War* beautifully portrays the central paradox of the gospel. If we take the words of the gospel to heart, she writes, we will find our true identity as an authentic people of God.

> But friends, it may not be that way. If you ask for the heart of Christ, yours may be broken. If you ask for the eyes of Christ, you may be horrified at what you see. If you try to embrace all mankind, as Christ did, you may be consumed by that love. Touching broken lives means to be touched back by the world's misery. The healer risks infection. The diseases are fear, loneliness, even insanity. If we fight injustice, we are identified with the condemned. We will bear about in our bodies the paradoxes of mankind, the yeas and nays.
>
> To be a Christian in the truest sense may mean to live on the edge of a cliff, shocked and dismayed at our own weaknesses, failure and evil. We go there as pilgrims and pioneers, and only God can keep us safe on that wild frontier.[1]

Notes

1. Shirley Nelson, *The Last Year of the War* (New York: Harper & Row, 1978), pp. 202-3.

MAJORITY AND MINORITY: HOW THE TWO CAN COEXIST

(For Cabinet Members)

Appointments are an opportunity for the bishop's cabinet to create an environment where minority pastors can make a difference. Such an environment requires attention to detail. This requires goal-oriented leadership on the part of the cabinet, a sense of urgency, and the ability to manage priorities. A creative bishop and an innovative cabinet can do a lot to set the stage for a positive atmosphere, but others (e.g., BOOM, SPRC, DCOM) must also do their part. The following areas of concern must be considered when cross-racial and cross-cultural appointments are made.

Psychological Support

Church ministry without skill and commitment takes pastors and churches nowhere. Early on, pastors from other cultures must realize that only those who are disciplined enough to know the language, dedicated enough to understand the culture, serious enough to comprehend the local environment, and eager enough to build and improve the art of communication will be able to have a sustained ministry in the local church. Noted author H. Jackson Brown said, "Talent without discipline is like an octopus on roller skates. There is plenty of movement, but you never know if it's going to be forward, backwards, or sideways."

Too often, ethnic-minority pastors are caught between *global-cultural behavior* and *North American-Anglo-cultural behavior*. Behavior that works for Anglos may not work for minority and ethnic-minority pastors. ethnic-minority pastors are often expected to break out of their cultural shell and develop or learn the culture of the people whom they serve. This cannot be done overnight. It takes time and persistence, and demands a willingness to learn.

Some ethnic-minority pastors are unaware of American cultural expectations, because they are new immigrants or newly arrived from urban seminaries where they have lived among their own friends and family. Too often their first appointment either makes or breaks them with little margin for error. Hence, there is a need for continual support and encouragement from the BOOM, DCOM, and leaders of the church to ensure that these pastoral candidates have a full grasp of American cultural and linguistic expectations. Lowering expectations and standards for these candidates only serves to harm these pastors and their congregations. Those lacking appropriate experience and skills should be required to attend classes at local colleges, seminaries, or universities, or work with private tutors until they demonstrate the necessary linguistic and communicative abilities.

Pastors are generalists not specialists. They are expected to know a little about many things. ethnic-minority pastors often benefit from continuing education courses on American culture, history, and religions and cults.

Church leaders must be aware that ethnic-minority pastors express emotional frustrations differently than their American counterparts. What may appear as frightening or dysfunctional to Americans may in fact be the results of feeling helpless or lost in an unfamiliar and strange church system.

Isolation and lack of fellowship with other minority or ethnic-minority pastors can make the initial adjustment to pastoral ministry more difficult for some. Hence, a single appointment in a district can result in disastrous consequences for ethnic and minority pastors. Without friendship or support from other minority and ethnic-minority pastors in similar situations, some pastors can become hostile and withdrawn.

At times, minority and ethnic-minority pastors are considered hostile *lone rangers* because they cut themselves off from their colleagues. However, behind the exterior of these soloists there is often anger and frustration at their inability to get support and cooperation from the congregation and their colleagues. Faced with a stone wall of resistance, they choose a path of least resistance—to go it alone.

Since few role models exist many ethnic-minority pastors assume they will be limited to smaller churches and rural congregations. This can create a major problem since in some cultures, particularly Asian countries, academic credentials are more highly valued than demonstrable skill and abilities. Pastors from these cultures often harbor high expectations about continually moving to larger, suburban churches. When they see colleagues from their home countries only pastoring smaller churches, they assume that they are destined for smaller churches as well. ethnic-minority pastors need assurance and guidance that ministry in a small congregation allows them to demonstrate their abilities to work within mainstream culture.

Too often, ethnic and minority pastors are excluded from collegial social outings and gatherings, so they tend to travel to socialize and associate with others of their ethnic origin.

Few minority and ethnic-minority pastors hold significant positions in Annual Conferences or denominational agencies. Those who do, however, too often pay dearly emotionally and physically.

Most minority and ethnic-minority pastors do not have seminary preparation or pastoral experience in cross-racial and cross-cultural ministry. The same is also true of Anglo pastors. However, "white privilege" allows for a wide range of behavioral styles. Conversely, a minority or ethnic-minority pastor's entire ministry often revolves around his or her success at one type of behavioral style. These pastors walk a tightrope in this area that places them in a do-or-die situation for success in ministry.

Fitting In vs Filling In

For minority and ethnic-minority pastors accepting a pastoral charge and moving to a new community, *fitting in* their new community is more important than *filling in* the pulpit. Unfortunately, they must deal with barriers that come in many forms and shapes. However, fitting in is critical because failing to do so will determine the future of the ministry in that congregation.

A relocation or transfer appointment to an area or region where no other minority or ethnic-minority pastors live can be particularly disconcerting. Being mindful of the sensitivity surrounding this situation will help leaders avoid sending minority or ethnic-minority pastors to a church or community indiscriminately.

Educating the congregation plays a crucial role in the success of cross-racial and cross-cultural appointments. Members of local churches are frequently influenced by people in the community. Through interactions in coffee shops and social gatherings, church members express their true feelings concerning cross-racial and cross-cultural appointments that can either help or hinder a pastorate.

Typically, the lack of job and educational opportunities results in few new families moving into rural and small town communities. For the most part, these communities are monoethnic with little or no ethnic diversity. When considering cross-racial and cross-cultural appointments in these communities, adequate preparation of the congregation and pastor is essential. Such a situation demands the full cooperation of the local church and the appointed pastor to work together as a team.

The Cabinet's Role

One thing that the minority and ethnic-minority pastors need and expect from the cabinet members is *help*, not ministerial aid or professional assistance. Aid implies weakness on the part of the one helped, while assistance relates to a secondary role on the part of the one offering the help. Although the cabinet cannot right a wrong, or respond to every need, they can:

- Accomplish a great deal with collaboration and cooperation by networking unceasingly to ensure that the cabinet and pastors stay informed and "in training" concerning cross-racial and cross-cultural ministry. This practice helps administrators and colleagues readily respond to emergency and crisis situations, as well as address short-term and long-term problems.
- Form successful partnerships through mentors and cluster groups that are available to help pastors during difficult situations. Moreover, initiating and implementing training and orientation sessions is also needed.
- Believe that solutions can be found, and this area of ministry can be effective.

Although cross-cultural and cross-racial appointments are challenging, the satisfaction of being in mission and ministry with God's people is well worth the effort.

Mission in Mutuality

When I was introduced to the SPRC at the historic African American St. Mark's UMC in Montclair, New Jersey, a committee member asked a surprise question concerning my cultural competence to pastor the congregation effectively. The questioner did not assume that my blackness automatically qualified me to pastor the congregation. Perhaps his real concern was whether or not my pastoral experiences in Anglo congregations had tainted my mind and soul beyond repair. His real question was this: *Can you lead this congregation effectively and maintain its style of worship while preserving its history and traditions?*

After pondering his query for a moment I responded by pointing out that I was born and nurtured in the African American church. My cultural heritage is the African American church, where I answered the call to ministry. I further pointed out that my first pastoral appointment was in an African American congregation. His concern was triggered by the fact that I would be coming to his congregation from an Anglo congregation.

I wanted him to know that my cross-cultural pastoral experiences over the years had helped me to learn more about ministry and to grow in Jesus Christ. This gift hopefully would also be a gift to the St. Mark's congregation.

What gifts will a pastor bring to our congregation? This is the haunting question asked by the SPRC at the time of an appointment change. It is not a question that is asked exclusively by majority congregations. Congregations want to know whether or not the pastor is culturally competent. Cultural competence supercedes the issue of race and ethnicity.

(ESL)

Chapter 9

Addressing Racism and Playing It Safe

(For Cabinet Members)

A recent radio commercial said, "The greatest risk is not taking one." Christian history does not contain stories of those who played it safe. Yet that is what most churches and leaders often do. From the beginning of Christianity, church history recounts that there were always temptations and attractions for following Jesus to sidestep. Perhaps, because of that, there is also something in us that admires the risktakers, the courageous, the ones who stand for conviction, the prophets and the seers, or the just and the bold who never wavered.

Sir Francis Bacon's friends often held ideas that troubled him deeply. He called those ideas "idols of tribe, the den, the market, and the theater." They represented, respectively, the *group think* of a particular community, the qualities of a particular individual, the result of social interaction, and the drama of showing off one's particular prowess.[1]

Only a few Christian denominations have the resources and power of The United Methodist Church. The bishops, cabinet members, BOOM, and DCOM have the power and authority to select, train, empower, and send candidates to serve local churches.

Even after making all the right moves, meeting all the credentials, and fulfilling all the requirements, ultimately only the bishops and their cabinets hold the key that unlocks the door for minority and ethnic-minority pastors to enter into pastoral ministry.

Facing the Challenge

Cross-racial and cross-cultural appointments are full of risks and apprehension on many sides: the *sender*, *sent*, and *receiver*. Hence, many who are involved in this process are motivated by fear, anxiety, and self-preservation. They fail to acknowledge that we all are foreigners in this present world. Unfortunately, many of us have gotten too comfortable with this world.

Regrettably, some pastors who have held certain prejudices all their lives carry stereotypes and preconceptions into the cabinet when they are appointed to serve as superintendents—hence the need to offer mandatory diversity, multicultural, and racism workshops at least once every two years for all pastors, especially cabinet and Board of Ordained Ministry members. The degree to which cabinet members are willing to take risks and empower minorities and ethnic minorities illustrates their sincerity in appreciating and fostering cross-racial and cross-cultural appointments.

Sweeping Race under the Rug

Cross-racial and cross-cultural appointments have several dimensions—*culture, race, education,* and *competency.* Moreover, they all need to function together. If, however, they are considered as one integral whole, inevitably they will clash and crash. Hence, there is a need to balance these dimensions through a shared awareness of how the parts function in harmony and interact with each other to produce the intended result. Although this is a high expectation, it can be accomplished.

The cabinet must begin making cross-racial and cross-cultural appointments by being cognizant of race, culture, class, and gender. Churches and their leaders are comprised of people who represent a society contaminated by racism, polluted by prejudice, and corrupted by stereotypes. This contamination pervades every walk of life, while hampering and stifling the full expression of a human being.

Cabinet members must be proactive, and recognize and identify the subtle and overt racial and other hostilities that exist. An awareness of the language that is used is critical. Vocabulary such as "we," "our," "us," and "American" or "he or she," "they," "their country," "their culture," and so forth, during discussions is problematic. Many pastors and laity fear plain talk about race relations, and thus hesitate to speak their minds. However, we must not cringe from race issues, but face them. The human species is divided into two genders and many races. Racial discrimination is as vicious as gender discrimination. However, minority and ethnic-minority female ministers and Anglo female ministers do not enjoy equal privileged status. Although some may refuse to accept it, the reality is white females are more privileged than non-white men and women. Whiteness carries its own privilege, be it male or female.

Furthermore, *racial diversity* and *diversity within a particular culture* should not be used interchangeably. Racism is filled with oppression, exploitation, and discrimination. In the ministerial context, racism undermines the potential for trust, acceptance, and effective engagement in God's mission. Unfortunately, the terms *racial diversity* and *diversity within a particular culture* are confused, and at times placed alongside *inclusion, pluralism,* and *multiculturalism.* We must exercise caution in not confusing race relations with matters of diversity.

Every church has some degree of *diversity* within its composition: men and women, rich and poor, educated and not-so-educated, gold-collar workers and blue-collar workers (see Galatians 3:8). Such diversity within a particular culture does not necessarily include racial inclusiveness and cultural incorporation. For the most part, it may contain a monoethnic group that has different levels of class and status, which are defined primarily by their socializing factors or functions. This type of diversity should not be seen as racial exclusivity or ethnocentric protectionism, but rather as a local church's satisfaction with its own particularity and the church leadership's lack of understanding of the larger picture. Although addressing classism is important, this manual is primarily concerned with minority and ethnic-minority ministers' identity, survival, and ministry in mainstream culture.

The larger picture of the society clearly shows the presence of racism and hostility in many churches and communities. Some church leaders even consider pastors who come from *the outside* as unsuitable for ministry within the church. Still others do not believe in "itinerant" ministry at all. Although mistakes and failures in God's mission can be sustained by God's abundant grace and mercy, denial and refusal of God's global and inclusive mission distorts the purpose and foundation of Christ's church on earth.

The Tie That Binds

Episcopal leadership begins in the Cabinet, where the bishop is the spiritual leader. The Cabinet, which is a fellowship of leaders and believers, spends significant amounts of time in worship. I believe that we experience Christian fellowship as we lean on Jesus together.

In our Cabinet we always have a prayer time, when we name all of our individual prayer concerns. We ask God to touch the named persons and make them whole according to God's will. We see ourselves as part of the whole family of believers, lay and clergy, who are part of the New York Annual Conference family. We always pray for discernment, especially with regard to appointment-making. We ask God to give us wisdom, insight, and the courage to be faithful disciples.

A few years ago, the entire Cabinet completed *Disciple I* in its entirety. We devoted 2½ hours of each Cabinet meeting to this very meaningful and beneficial enterprise. It was an effort to discern the meaning of our own discipleship, as well as a means of further uniting us in spiritual partnership with God and with each other. This process of building discipleship brought us into a more intimate spiritual relationship with the laity and clergy.

Our effort to discern God's yearnings is not individualistic, but collective. So we ask the question, what is God's yearning for this Conference in a multicultural society? We know for sure that we are bound together in Christian love with all of our brothers and sisters regardless of their race or culture. This is the tie that binds. It is God's rainbow.

Notes

1. Kawasaki, *Rules of Revolutionaries* (New York: Harper and Row, 1959), p. 6.

CHAPTER 10

THE CABINET AND MINORITY PASTORS

(For Cabinet Members)

Numerous boundaries divide the American society in general, and The United Methodist Church in particular. Among these boundaries are race, ethnicity, class, culture, gender, and other divisions that separate members of the human family. God, however, crosses these boundaries and invites all pilgrim disciples to follow in the footsteps of Jesus.

Jesus, a radical with no fear of boundaries, whether cultural or religious, commissioned the disciples to cross boundaries as he had taught them to do during their in-service training with him: "Go therefore and make disciples of all nations" (Matthew 28:19a). The teachings and examples of Jesus are at the heart of our mission theology, which guides ministry in a multicultural world.

John Wesley said, "The world is my parish." He meant that no boundaries, geographical or otherwise, would limit his preaching the good news of Jesus Christ. Wesley went anywhere people were willing to listen to him preach. He was not, however, always received with a warm welcome in every place. Nonetheless, he went to the margins of society and ministered among the poor in the name of Jesus.

Minority and ethnic-minority pastors are a part of God's mission in the world. In the context of the UMC, some minority and ethnic-minority pastors are called to serve in ministry with majority congregations. Moreover, some majority congregations are asked to receive a pastor who comes from a culture other than their own. Some majority pastors are asked to serve in minority and ethnic-minority congregations. The cross-cultural and cross-racial pastoral appointment constitutes *Many Faces, One Church*. As the guardians of the appointment process, the cabinet has certain responsibilities and opportunities. Cabinet members are charged with the responsibility of facilitating the appointment system. In addition, the cabinet has the opportunity to create a context/atmosphere in which cross-cultural and cross-racial appointments can occur and succeed.

The *Social Principles* points out that *racism includes both personal and institutional racism* (*The Book of Discipline 2004,* ¶162 A). This same paragraph continues with the following statement:

> Personal racism is manifested through the individual expressions, attitudes, and/or behaviors that accept the assumptions of a racist value system and that maintain the benefits of this system. Institutional racism is the established social pattern that supports implicitly or explicitly the racist value system. Racism plagues and cripples our growth in Christ, inasmuch as it is antithetical to the gospel itself. White people are unfairly granted privileges and benefits that are denied to persons of color. Therefore, we recognize racism as sin and affirm the ultimate and temporal worth of all persons. We rejoice in the gifts that particular ethnic histories and cultures bring to our total life.

The above characterizes a truth about American society that is also applicable to The United Methodist Church, its Annual Conferences, districts, and local congregations. Racism is present in the greater society and within the Church.

When we consider the presence of racism, the UMC has a clear standard with regard to appointment-making and open itineracy:

> Clergy shall be appointed by the bishop, who is empowered to make and fix all appointments in the episcopal area of which the annual conference is a part. Appointments are to be made with consideration of the gifts and evidence of God's grace of those appointed, to the needs, characteristics, and opportunities of congregations and institutions, and with faithfulness to the commitment to an open itineracy. Open itineracy means appointments are made without regard to race, ethnic origin, gender, color, disability, marital status, or age, except for the provisions of mandatory retirement through appointment-making, the connectional nature of The United Methodist system is made visible. (*The Book Of Discipline 2000,* ¶430.1)

Not only must the Cabinet lift high this standard, but they must also adhere to it and cultivate a climate where cross-cultural and cross-racial appointments are a meaningful reality for the pastor, his or her family, and the congregation.

The General Commission on Religion and Race provides assistance in this endeavor. First, the Commission works with Annual Conferences in doing an assessment of conditions regarding the varied manifestations/results of institutional racism in an Annual Conference. Second, the Commission conducts workshops on cross-racial and cross-cultural appointments for the Cabinet and other parties, such as the Staff-Parish Relations Committee. Such workshops help bishops and district superintendents confront their own personal racism and prejudices, and identify their level of cultural competence.

Each resident bishop has the responsibility to provide leadership in implementing open itineracy. The bishop provides the impetus and sparks the initiative of the Annual Conference. This is done primarily through his or her work with and within the Cabinet, but not exclusively. Each district superintendent can take the initiative in his or her district by conducting district-wide racism seminars. They can also promote programming that supports the increase of cultural competence among clergy and laity, Staff-Parish Relations Committees, and congregations.

The SPRC and the local church pastor, working together, have the responsibility and opportunity to prepare a congregation to receive a cross-cultural or cross-racial appointment at some point in the future. The following are several options that are applicable to all congregations, regardless of race or ethnicity:

- The SPRC can begin with itself by engaging in self-reflection and training about the issues and dynamics of racism, white privilege, and committee members' cultural competence.
- Working with the Administrative Council, the SPRC can provide the congregation with opportunities to engage in self-reflection and training about the issues and dynamics of racism, white privilege, and its own cultural competence.
- A congregation can seek appropriate ways to cooperate in ministry and mission with a neighboring congregation of a different racial or ethnic group (e.g., joint Vacation Bible School, adult education seminars, joint worship services, shared mission projects, joint volunteer in mission opportunities).
- The SPRC can indicate to the district superintendent the congregation's willingness to receive a cross-cultural or cross-racial appointment.
- The congregation can engage in prayer and appropriate Bible study.

Each Annual Conference can help congregations prepare for this type of ministry by developing a set of guidelines for cross-cultural or cross-racial appointment-making. Bishops, cabinets, Staff-Parish Relations Committees, congregations, and seminaries must begin working together to prepare culturally competent ministers and congregations who will welcome open itinerary.

The above preparation is a prelude to bridging the crossing point, that is, moving from cultural incompetence to cultural competence, and moving from cultural and racial exclusiveness to racial and cultural inclusivity. While resident bishops must lead this transformation, Cabinet members must guide the process to the places where the Holy Spirit is creating new ministries at the crossing point. The Conference Board of Ordained Ministry and the District Committees on Ordained Ministry must be in partnership with the bishop and Cabinet, as well as with pastors and congregations.

Careful Listening Bears Fruit

Dropping in for Sunday worship was always a delightful experience for me. I liked to hang out during the fellowship hour after the worship service. One Sunday morning I visited a congregation that was in the first year of a cross-cultural pastoral appointment. The new pastor was an excellent pastoral leader with previous experience in a cross-cultural appointment. As I lingered, an older man approached me and expressed appreciation for his pastor. He shared that he was getting more out of the new pastor's sermons than he could ever remember getting out of sermons during recent years. His statement, however, was not a negative reflection on his several pastors.

I asked the man why this was the case. His response was twofold. First, he admitted that his hearing was not good. Second, he confessed that it was difficult to understand the pastor, who had a pronounced accent that he was unaccustomed to hearing. Because of these two realities, he confessed that he listened with greater intentionality and focus. In other words, he paid attention to his pastor's sermons so that he could hear them and understand each word. This attentive listening led him to experience new depths of understanding. His careful listening bore the fruit of understanding.

(ESL)

CHAPTER 11

LIVING THE HALLMARKS OF LEADERSHIP

(For Cabinet Members)

Taking Risks and Trying New Things

Often the choice of district superintendents and the appointment methods of the cabinets set the tone and direction of the Annual Conferences' ministerial future. Bishops act as role models, and cabinet members follow suit. District Superintendents, in turn, encourage the key qualities needed for effectiveness in local churches. Thus a top-down, cascading current of responsibility, motivation, encouragement, and assuring presence flows throughout the conference.

As a result, the composition of the cabinet is critical. In particular, cross-racial and cross-cultural representation is needed on the cabinet to foster fresh insights that offer a comprehensive view of the conference and ministry. Only through such diversity will this team have the knowledge and ability to take the required steps that will yield measurable benefits. After all, diversity enhances creativity and innovation in ministry.

The composition of the cabinet reflects the bishop's vision for the conference. A wholistic cabinet includes a variety of perspectives such as: laity, women, minority, ethnic-minority, as well as future possibilities. District Superintendents must be able to meet the professional needs of pastors and quickly grasp the larger picture of a conference, community, and congregation, while also facing the challenges of nontraditional appointments.

Mission-Driven and Globally Connected

The role of the office of superintendency is not merely about connection, but it also relates to *cooperation* and *collaboration*. Although a pastor is visible and active in district and conference activities, he or she may not be well suited as a district superintendent. An effective superintendent is one who has *experienced cultural and mental transformation, the desire to change and transcend established standards and expectations, a* high tolerance for ambiguity, an openness for pastors with varying opinions of ministries, and the ability to take action, set goals, and measure values not only from a majority yardstick but also from the minority perspective. In short, a superintendent needs to undergo an emotional, psychological, and professional cycle of change before any actual administrative work can occur.

Regrettably, not all district superintendents are open to cross-racial and cross-cultural appointments because they fear taking an ecclesiastical risk or an institutional chance. Some have heard horror stories about a few failed CR/CC appointments and use them as an excuse not to make such appointments. Their voices join with the fearful saying, "Congregations are not ready yet. Let's wait for a year or two to make sure." Conversely, others listen to the attributes of minority and ethnic-minority pastors and readily take chances in making more appointments. Too often the former is the experience of minority and ethnic-minority pastors.

Sam Walton, the founder of Wal-Mart, once said: "I guess in all my years, what I heard more often than anything was: a town of less than 50,000 population cannot support a discount store for very long."[1] Few are born to take this kind of risk. Leadership for the missional journey is no exception. However, if Christian mission is "an enterprise," then church leaders can learn from their secular counterparts who long ago discovered that the way to succeed is to take risks. Cross-racial and cross-cultural appointments certainly involve risk-taking. Cabinets, district superintendents, or congregations can no longer remain neutral. It is time to take the risk, particularly in a denomination that values connectionalism.

Given their spiritual maturity and missiological involvement, some district superintendents are broadminded and open hearted, while others are quite closed and deeply prejudiced. Most people, though, grow into this role of supervisor and discover methods and techniques that develop their leadership skills and broaden their view of mission and ministry. During their growth process, some district superintendents may even establish a strong solidarity with others who have been negatively affected by gender, race, and cultural difference. On the other hand, others shy away from interaction with strangers unfamiliar with "American" culture. They fear that these strangers, who do not know the local culture and language, will harm the church's membership, damage congregations, and generate unnecessary problems.

The way a cabinet member responds to D. H. Lawrence's poem illustrates the level of commitment he or she may have for United Methodist connectionalism and global Christianity.

Not I, not I, but the wind that blows through me!
A fine wind is blowing a new direction of Time.
If only I let it bear me, carry me, if only it carry me!
If only I am sensitive, subtle, oh, delicate, a winged gift!
If only, most lovely of all, I yield myself and am borrowed
By the fine, fine wind that takes its course thorough the chaos of the world
Like a fine exquisite chisel, a wedge blade inserted;
If only I am keen and hard like the sheer tip of a wedge
Driven by invisible blows,

The Rock will split, we shall come at the wonders, we shall find the Hesperides.
Oh, for the wonder that bubbles in my soul,
Would be a good fountain, a good well-head,
Would blur no whisper, spoil no expression.
What is the knocking?
What is the knocking at the door in the night?
It is somebody wants to do us harm.
No, no, it is three strange angels.
Admit them, admit them.[2]

Embracing Change and Encouraging Excellence

Ensuring that cross-racial and cross-cultural appointments succeed is a joint effort shared by district superintendents and local churches. Every effort must be made to integrate the leadership and ministry, and responses and resources of both sides. This can only be achieved through divine wisdom, human collaboration, and multicultural management skill.

District Superintendents who do not support cross-racial and cross-cultural appointments thwart the vision of The United Methodist Church as a connectional church and its appointment system. One way to avoid such a situation is to ask prospective superintendents about their views on cross-racial and cross-cultural appointments. District Superintendents must be willing to build a long-term professional and ministerial partnership with minority and ethnic-minority pastors. During that process, they must be willing to relate personally to minority and ethnic-minority pastors, and to help channel the intellectual and emotional energies and creativity of minority pastors.

Many cross-racial and cross-cultural appointments fail as a result of prejudice, non-cooperation, and exclusion, which only serve to create tension and anxiety for the pastor and his or her family. Anxiety is contagious. Minority and ethnic-minority family members suffer together. At times, families break up, or relationships within families become strained. Without adequate support and nurturing, too many of them will continue to scream in silence.

If the church's leadership is truly concerned about saving families, then pastors and their families serving in cross-racial and cross-cultural appointments must also be added to the list. Some pastors suffer needlessly in the hands of untrained leaders in the local church *and* in the cabinet. Just as the cabinet searches for effective pastors to provide leadership in congregations, bishops must also look for effective superintendents to provide leadership for pastors.

District superintendents are in the advantageous position of being able to address problems as they arise. They have the administrative authority to intervene and moral capacity to create a healthy, collaborative environment between pastors and congregations. However, if superintendents are expected to respond to issues arising out of cross-racial and cross-cultural appointments, they must have a broader knowledge base than church administration. They must be cross-disciplined. Those who are untrained and unaware of the dynamics of multicultural management will only exacerbate the problems faced by churches and their minority pastors.

Finally, district superintendents who truly want to serve as pastors of pastors must expand their hearts and minds to leviathan proportion by coming to appreciate other cultures and races, and develop a love for the global church.

Notes

1. Quoted by Kawasaki, *Rules of Revolutionaries* p. 24.
2. D. H. Lawrence, *Selected Poems* (New York: Viking Press, 1959), p. 74.

CHAPTER 12

RACISM AND THE CHURCH

(For District Superintendents, Board of Ordained Ministry, and Staff-Parish Relations Committee)

Cabinet members who expect minority and ethnic-minority pastors to excel in their appointments too often ignore the pernicious effects of racism and non-cooperation that occurs in local communities and churches. More often than not, no protection or emotional support is provided for pastors serving in cross-racial and cross-cultural contexts. Additionally, little or no preparation or groundwork has been provided that would help such a partnership succeed.

Denominational leaders and officials must be aware of and acknowledge the reality of racial prejudice within the Christian community in rural and urban settings. Since many minority and ethnic-minority ministers pastor in rural areas, special efforts must be made to understand the racial dynamics that operate in rural areas. Racism is alive and deeply entrenched in some rural churches and communities, and is often combined with fierce geographic and community loyalties. Pastors who fail to fit the norm and standards of the local community are sometimes severely reprimanded. Moreover, often community concerns significantly impact the life of the church, and the pastor and church are expected to respond.

Steps of Preparation

Sadly, minorities and ethnic minorities are often saddled with offensive stereotypes that negatively affect their ministry. Hence it is paramount to note that racism frequently impedes success and progress in ministry. Many ethnic-minority pastors enter ministry with no awareness of racism, ageism, or the other host of *isms* that exist. When they encounter such "isms," they become apprehensive and fearful about expressing their true feelings. Self-doubt and lack of confidence haunt them, and they often become depressed and withdrawn. By asking pastors to talk about their experiences and prompting them for their side of the story, leaders help to heal their self-doubt.

Ethnic-minority pastors who are recent immigrants to America have lived alongside people of other faiths in their birth countries, and have often been persecuted or discriminated against. In America, though, they are often baffled and confused when they encounter a different type of discrimination, one that is based on race or ethnic origin. The Anglo missionaries who shared the gospel with them in their birth countries said nothing about the sins of racism and prejudice based on one's skin color.

As a result, the cabinet, in collaboration with the Board of Ordained Ministry and SPRC, needs to address this problem by creating an environment that is supportive and trustworthy. Moreover, this environment should be one in which both the foreign-born and native-born minority and ethnic-minority pastors can open their hearts without reservation to express their confusion, fear, and anger. Such an environment will help to validate, empower, and heal minority and ethnic-minority pastors and their ministries.

Entry-level minority and ethnic-minority pastors must be nurtured with sensitivity and skillful support as so much depends on first appointment. District superintendents must be intentional in their efforts to help ethnic-minority pastors succeed. One way that is helpful is to provide them with mentors. Additionally, supervisors need to be mindful that many minority and ethnic-minority pastors experience stress, fear, and apprehension about serving a congregation with a different cultural or racial makeup. A fear of rejection based on race may even dominate their ministries. When pastors operate from fear and non-acceptance, they are not able to minister well. Dreams and visions become casualties in such an environment.

A study commissioned by the Division of Ordained Ministry of the General Board of Higher Education details the above further:

> Ethnic-minority pastors are often concerned with how they are perceived by their colleagues, by the hierarchy, and by their congregations. This includes how they are being received, how they come across, and whether others accept them or reject them. This concern about the perception of others tends to be exacerbated by a strong conscience, high moral values, and zealousness. Idealism and intelligence further contribute to the unrealistic expectations that pastors have of themselves and sometimes of others. Indeed, some pastors drive themselves unnecessarily, sometimes even mercilessly; it can be said that there are factors both within and without that evoke within ministers feelings of not doing enough. Along with their other pressures, clergy experience these self-expectations with differing intensity. However, they are not always willing to talk about their problems; when there is a willingness, they do not always find a responsive setting outside the family context in which they can confide.[1]

As a rule of thumb, leaders should avoid appointing minority and ethnic-minority pastors to churches or communities where a cloud of hostility exists. In such a situation, no ministry or program can take root and grow. The best course of action in such situations is to spend several months or even years preparing the congregation and community for a coming appointment through spiritual, missional, and biblical education.

Sometimes international political and economic events can also have an effect on the ministries of ethnic-minority pastors. For example, U.S. foreign policy against the birth country of minority pastors will subtly or overtly impact their ministries in a local church.

Some minority and ethnic-minority pastors are naive about subtle racism in the church and among their colleagues since they have never been trained on how to deal with prejudices within the church. Even as they feel the power of racism and experience its unpleasant effects, they find it hard to name and address it. Worst of all, they are often unable to identify the sources of their racial and noncooperation problems. In dealing with such problems, some ethnic minorities are culturally passive.

However, this passiveness should not be interpreted as having no feelings. Unfortunately, even in light of years of pastoral experience, minority and ethnic-minority pastors are asked repeatedly to prove their credibility in direct and indirect ways, both by denominational leadership and church members. Often they have to interpret and translate every idea they want to initiate in the congregation. In addition, minority and ethnic-minority pastors are evaluated more harshly than their Anglo counterparts.

As indicated above, often minority and ethnic-minority pastors suffer and grieve about racism in silence. In many cases, the only people they share their true feelings with are their spouses and children. The emotional price they pay to succeed in ministry is immeasurable personally and on their families. A common problem among some ethnic-minority pastors is the guilt and loneliness they experience when their churches lose membership and struggle financially. Some are too ashamed to talk about it, and will only open up to those they trust. Aloofness and withdrawal are signs that these pastors need encouragement to seek collegial and professional help.

The central issue for a sizeable number of ethnic-minority persons is *not* job or career success, but survival in a culture that is foreign to them. In addition, it is about economically providing enough for their families, and personally finding a deeper sense of worth and belonging. Too many ethnic-minority pastors living in America are torn inside and out. Their children are not accepted by the dominant culture and are also marginalized by their own ethnic groups. The alienation of the pastor, and her or his spouse and children, is a critical problem that must be addressed if the church is to achieve true Christian fellowship.

The Subtlety of Racism

Racism often has a subtle way of manifesting itself, even among faithful laity and clergy. Let us consider an all-too-frequent example that I have noticed over the many years of attending district, conference, and cabinet meetings. It is the reality of restricted relationships, which limits a person's knowledge about a cross section of people in the Annual Conference. When it comes time to nominate a person for membership on a committee or board or for appointment consideration, the people at the table often are restricted to their circle of friends and acquaintances. Our personal circle is often confined to people who are like us, members of our own cultural or racial group. This is a matter of cultural competence. Too often, the names of racial/ethnic persons are considered almost as an afterthought. Is this an example of racism, even though subtle?

(ESL)

Notes

1. *One Household*, p. 24.

PREVENTION AND INTERVENTION

(For District Superintendents)

I n cross-racial and cross-cultural appointments the major struggle is the management of a new, dynamic ministry. The routine mechanistic and traditional models will not work here. Seminary, BOOM, Cabinet, SPRC, and DCOM must come together to more appropriately prepare pastors for these appointments. Integration is the foundation for effectiveness in any field of service. At present, there is a radical disconnect between seminary training and church ministry. Just as the pieces of a puzzle must be coordinated, so too do the various players in ministry (i.e., seminary, BOOM, Cabinet, SPRC, and DCOM) need to be carefully and thoughtfully put together. The goal must be to teach all parties involved to think and work together strategically. As concerns are recognized, appropriate parties must be prepared to address problems at all levels from preparation to appointments.

Inexplicably, in some conferences, before and after an appointment of a pastor from another culture is made, the SPRC and congregation are put on hold. Consequently, when problems arise during the process the message being sent is, "We are busy figuring out the solutions, and will let you know when we are ready." The current process of making CR/CC appointments in The United Methodist Church resembles undergoing five medical procedures at the same time. One person is doing laser eye surgery, the second is doing a root canal, a third is doing a laparoscopy, a fourth is working on dialysis, and the fifth person is replacing a broken knee. Imagine in the midst of all this the electricity going off and the patient dying of shock. Too much is happening at one time.

Just as with any appointments, when making cross-racial and cross-cultural appointments, leaders must recognize and acknowledge concerns, as well as anticipate and be prepared to address problems. The following are several suggestions that can be used as a starting point to finding solutions to various problems:

Managing Crises

Avoid stepping in to perform the ministerial tasks (e.g., baptisms, weddings, or funerals) in times of crisis, but instead empower the pastor by following denominational, conference, and cabinet policy. Suppress the temptation to act like an ecclesiastical messiah, for it is dysfunctional rescue.

Allow minority and ethnic-minority pastors time to grow. Racism and discrimination may temporarily stun the effectiveness of pastors, but after overcoming the hostile situation and getting a handle on various problems, the church will grow and their ministry will flourish. During times of hostility, pastors need support, encouragement, and direction.

Identify a comprehensive, as well as focused, approach to addressing oppression with congregations and the larger church. One form of racism or oppression does not take precedence over another. All forms of oppression dehumanize and destroy a pastor's effectiveness. Elimination of one form of oppression is a good starting point, but the continued presence of others will continue to wreak havoc and destruction.

Provide psychic and professional support. Unfortunately, fellow pastors who are Anglo cannot provide this type of support since minority pastors are generally expected by these colleagues to "become white like them." The irony of such an expectation is that minority pastors rarely know what "being white like them" is! Even if they tried to become so, the result would be disastrous.

Avoid making appointments if pastors are not able to function. This situation is simply a set-up for failure. Instead the superintendent needs to monitor her or his pastors' ministries, dialogue regularly with them, and offer encouragement and guidance when needed.

Visit minority and ethnic-minority pastors occasionally (what you don't inspect you don't respect). Empowerment does not mean abandonment.

Hold pastors accountable. Accountability makes it possible to be clear about what is happening in the local church. If the cabinet, pastor, and laity are clear about a pastor's responsibilities, later there will be no rude awakenings, surprises, finger pointing, or atmosphere of helplessness.

Provide feedback. Minority and ethnic-minority pastors want to know if they have not done a good job, and how they can do better. It helps when they are measured against appropriate norms or standards and can use this information to improve themselves. As Philip B. Crosby writes in *Quality Is Free*: "Improvement itself is never the real difficulty. Once individuals recognize and agree another position, it is never difficult to improve. The unfortunate part is that very few of us own up."[1]

Offer feedback during a face-to-face meeting to help develop a cooperative and partnership environment.

Confront ecclesiastical contentions. Doing so will lead to a creative process or destructive place. Be open, creating a win-win situation for everyone involved.

Ask the pastors and their families serving in cross-racial and cross-cultural contexts to share their personal feelings, phobias, experiences, and assumptions about ministry. Whenever possible, include spouses, since they can often provide a unique perspective. When you get together, show genuine concern. Ask them to air their feelings about concerns and conflict in the church and community.

Stay vigilant to potential problems, and address those that arise as quickly as possible.

Offer a strong stance against discrimination. Insist that such abusive behavior be stopped immediately.

Promote the message that the entire denomination, including every congregation and conference, is to engage in the task of eradicating discrimination within the church. Discrimination and racial harassment are social and spiritual problems, not isolated or individual ones.

Explore and identify how race, culture, and stereotypes influence conflict resolutions during times of crisis in a local church. Do not settle for quick fix methods. Instead search for the roots of conflict and address them. Such an action demands proficiency with details, as well as skill, in multicultural management.

Be aware that racism in a local church is about power and control. The SPRC and district superintendent play a major role in fostering cooperation between the pastor and the congregation to seek and maintain a relationship of mutuality, equality, and partnership in fulfilling the mission of the church.

Be alert to and prepared for difficulties after a minority or ethnic-minority pastor is appointed.

Include minorities and ethnic minorities in making major policy decisions that might impact their family and ministerial welfare, such as health benefits, pension benefits, and parsonage standards. Exclusion from majority decision-making breeds distrust.

Recognize that rectifying the wrongs experienced by minority and ethnic-minority pastors is a justice issue. The abused need advocacy and support, while the abuser deserves accountability and admonition.

Notes

1. Philip B. Crosby, *Quality Is Free* (New York: McGraw Hill, 1979), p. 52.

CHAPTER 14

WHEN TAKING MINORITY PASTORS TO MEET WITH SPRC

(For District Superintendents)

L
isted below are suggestions for district superintendents during the pastor's first meeting with the SPRC:

Define and explain the role of the SPRC so that members of the committee understand their role and the committee's responsibilities.

Avoid verbally or psychologically *handing over* a minority or ethnic-minority pastor to the chairperson or members of SPRC. Such an action construes that the chairperson or this group is the pastor's supervisor(s). Clarify the appointment process and explain the UMC's itinerant system.

Clarify the appointment system to the SPRC and clearly define the SPRC's role and responsibilities. This is critical, especially with cross-racial and cross-cultural appointments. The most important clarification that needs to be addressed is the SPRC's function as a liaison between the pastor and the church, and between the pastor and the cabinet.

Create, with the help of the SPRC, an environment that is conducive for minority pastors to succeed.

Avoid recommending or appointing a candidate to a church if you are opposed to cross-racial and cross-cultural appointments. You cannot convince others of something that you are not convinced about.

Ask yourself, *before* making a recommendation of cross-racial and cross-cultural appointment to the cabinet, the following questions:

- Is this an inclusive church?
- Is this a good church for a minority or ethnic-minority pastor?
- Can I sense and smell support and encouragement from the SPRC?
- How is salary compensation in comparison to an Anglo pastor who has the same number of years in ministry?

- Am I making this appointment because I could not find another pastor to serve this charge?
- Do I think minority and ethnic-minority pastors are only good for rural, multi-point, or inner-city churches?

Stick to your guns once the decision is made by the cabinet. Usually resistance to cross-racial and cross-cultural appointments surfaces a week or so after the announcement is made, and is accompanied by pleading for reconsideration.

Present a positive picture of minority and ethnic-minority pastors. Avoid giving a condescending or patronizing picture of the candidate. Some minority pastors tell horror stories about the way they were represented by their district superintendents during their introduction to the SPRC. One Korean pastor shared that when she was taken to a church by her DS, the SPRC refused to accept her as their pastor. While she was present, the DS said to the SPRC, "We cannot send her to any other church, *please* take her at least for a year." A Chinese pastor said that he was asked by the DS and the SPRC to go to the sanctuary and read selected passages from the scriptures, and was subjected to probing personal questions for over four hours.

Recognize and prevent bias and prejudicial questions in the meeting process no matter how innocently presented.

Moderate the meeting with warmth and care by steering away from questions that might create an embarrassing situation for the candidate or the SPRC.

Prepare the members of the SPRC just like any other appointments. However, additional groundwork will also be needed on behalf of minority and ethnic-minority pastors.

Identify areas of ministries that will build a strong, mutually enriching relationship. Also, explain the complexities of cross-racial and cross-cultural appointments such as: preaching with an accent, different modes of interpreting the Bible, new styles of communication, and varying models of administration. SPRC members may not be open to those new ideas and ways of church ministry. Herein the spadework begins! The church members need to be prepared with the knowledge that we are a global church and connectional church. Because of shortage of pastors and availability of pastors who are not from the same racial and/or cultural background, all churches need to be prepared for cross-racial and cross-cultural pastoral appointments.

Create and put in place a "fix-it" lifeline such as, "*When there is a lack of communication,*" "*In the event of misunderstanding,*" or "*In times of crisis*" contact. . . . In other words, both the district superintendent and members of the SPRC need to be proactive.

No Vacancy

When my wife, Glory, was appointed to the Women's Division of the General Board of Global Ministries of The United Methodist Church, I was working as a senior pastor of one of the largest congregations in Illinois Great Rivers Conference. In order for us to be closer together, I asked for a transfer appointment in seven different conferences on the east coast. Three bishops responded, saying no appointment was available. The other bishops did not even bother to respond to my request. After waiting a year, I pursued letter correspondences with two bishops whose jurisdictions were close to Glory's work place. The correspondences lasted for six years, and still *no vacancy!*

In the meantime, a district superintendent in one of the above conferences happened to travel on a bus with a good friend of mine, who was an Anglo and was working for the General Board of Global Ministries. The District Superintendent solicited my friend to serve as a pastor in his district. My friend was flattered! Then he asked the DS if he had received a transfer request from Jacob. When the DS responded affirmatively, my friend pleaded with him to give that appointment to me. The response: *no vacancy!*

I was devastated after hearing about the incident and wrote again to the Bishop of the DS's conference, pleading for a transfer appointment. *No vacancy!* Not being able to restrain myself, and after six years of correspondence, I wrote to the same Bishop, recounting the conversation between my friend and the DS. This time—no response!

Meanwhile, a man of God was chosen to episcopacy in New York Annual Conference. When he heard about our plight, and soon after assuming his responsibilities as episcopal leader, an appointment was given to me.

A few months after moving to the New York Annual Conference, I attended the clergy session held at the Memorial Church in White Plains. A member of the Board of Ordained Ministry gave a glowing report about the BOOM's effort, and his own travel to seminaries across the U.S., to recruit "qualified" pastors to serve in the New York Annual Conference.

Too often we overlook what is in our midst.

(JSD)

CHAPTER 15

REVIEWING MINORITY PASTORS

(For District Superintendents)

E ach year pastors and their ministries are assessed and evaluated by district super-intendents and SPRCs. Based on the information they collect, appointments are made for the upcoming year. Consequently, many Annual Conferences have a practice of sending annual review forms to pastors for self-evaluation and SPRCs for performance evaluation. Given the unique nature of cross-racial and cross-cultural ministry, the creation of a specially designed review form for minority and ethnic-minority pastors is warranted. The term *specially designed* does not mean low standard, but simply a different scale for evaluation.

The evaluation tool currently used by the majority of SPRCs for Anglo pastors works well, since they are familiar with its style and criteria. Conversely, the majority of ethnic-minority pastors use different styles of ministry, and, therefore, should be evaluated in a way that truly measures these pastor's gifts and skills, as well as the local church's ministry. In order to develop such an evaluation tool, cabinet members and SPRC members must learn multicultural management.

During the evaluation process, do not lump *all* minority and ethnic-minority pastors together as failures or successes. For instance, one Asian pastor does not represent all Asian pastors. Ethnicity is divided by race, language, and geography. African Americans and Anglos are categorized by race, Hispanics by language, and Asians by geography. Under each ethnicity or minority group, there are a number of sub-groups such as African American, Caribbean American, Native American, East-Indian American, and so on.

Church leaders need to be aware of existing internal and external barriers to minis-terial success for minority pastors. These barriers, along with other political bound-aries, contribute to and affect their ministries. Sensitivity to differences and learning how to communicate and review these pastors is what is needed. In order to transcend boundaries and overcome barriers, district superintendents and other leaders must be willing to look beyond narrow cultural boundaries and linguistic barriers. They also need to deepen their missional understanding and reflect upon unifying Christian principles that synthesize apparent dualities. After all, Christian ministry demands multiple points of presence.

One way to gain a greater understanding of minority and ethnic-minority pastors is to look at the church and its ministries through their eyes. In doing so, leaders may discover that what is considered normal or correct, may not be normal or correct to them. Imposing one group or community's standards upon another, and then evaluating that person's performance based on that standard is cultural violence and professional oppression.

Unfortunately, not all churches and their members are open to minority and ethnic-minority pastors' leadership and ministries. Consequently, they are not willing to collaborate, cooperate, or engage in the ministry within the local church. When this occurs it is the responsibility of the district superintendent to dialogue with the members of the SPRC about the pastor, the church, and a suitable evaluation method. The SPRC's review is an opportunity to assess both the pastor and the parish, individually and as a team. Each pastor brings his or her own unique style to ministry, which influences and encourages the church to flourish if love and acceptance are involved.

In reviewing the performance of a minority pastor, the process must be based on enhancing the effectiveness of the pastor, not simply determining how this stranger fits into the local church or community. Ultimately, the purpose of the review is to collaborate with and compliment the church and the pastor. This is *not* a time to point out deficits and weaknesses of the pastor or the church. The entire process should be a mutually agreed upon assessment of the pastor-church partnership.

In addition, the review process should feature a feedback system, where the pastor reviews the SPRC and the church, and the SPRC reviews the pastor, and missional goals and purpose as set by the church council or charge conference. If the process is to be truly beneficial, then the pastor must be given information about the criteria used for later evaluation. Hence, during the charge conference, the superintendent should encourage each church to set missional goals for the next year. As a result, the review should start with this information. Unfortunately, sometimes the SPRC review demoralizes and crushes the spirit of someone new to pastoral ministry. To avoid this situation, each conference should consider creating a review manual and organizing a training session for SPRC members where they learn constructive feedback methodology. An accompanying video featuring a mock-review is also an excellent resource. Reliance on the district annual training or orientation session is often inadequate and deficient for such a critical assessment.

A special focus of this training should be reviewing pastors who are culturally and racially different from the majority of the congregation. The review might also offer ways to improve, expand, and reward minority pastors, as well as celebrate their successes, for ministerial success is integrally tied to human respect and expressed emotions.

In addition, the review must be tied to salary increases and monetary compensation. Promotion and monetary rewards should be an incentive for faithfulness and effectiveness in ministry. When considering the annual review of the pastor and the church, the evaluation tool being used must be fair.

Unfortunately, in some churches pastors are tested and reviewed harshly. In these cases, many times the mundane day-to-day office routine can undermine the pastor's ministerial effectiveness more than her or his sacramental and caring ministries. Often, SPRC members bring a dualistic cultural or worldview to the review, looking for only two sides to every concern—a right side and a wrong side. They interpret church ministry from their perspective, defending what they consider *right* and attacking what is considered *wrong*. On the other hand, patience and an openness to understanding and accepting another's perspective is what is needed for an honest and true assessment to occur.

Questions for Reviewing Minority Pastors

1. What are your joys and concerns about cross-racial and cross-cultural appointments?
2. How do minority pastors respond to those "joys and concerns"?
3. Describe the morale of minority pastors in your conference or district?
4. Do you conduct education and awareness-building workshops?
5. When was the last time you spent one-on-one time with a minority pastor? Why? How did it go?
6. Is your cabinet's base diverse?
7. Do you believe in cross-racial and cross-cultural appointments? Why?
8. Do you believe that in the future the conference or district will utilize a more diverse clergy population?
9. Would you recommend your conference or district as a good place for cross-racial and cross-cultural candidates to pastor?
10. Do you perceive any missional advantages of making cross-racial and cross-cultural appointments?
11. Are there malcontents or majority pastors and churches that might create barriers to cross-racial pastors in performing ministries in your area?
12. Do you want minority pastors to serve in leadership roles of the conference or district?
13. Do you intentionally recruit minority pastors for such roles?
14. Are there stereotypes/perceptions of any minority pastors that might create resistance/barriers to growth and effectiveness?
15. Has your conference or district experienced problems resulting from cross-racial and cross-cultural appointments? What are they?
16. How many minority pastors serve as senior pastors in your conference or district? How many are in non-rural settings? How many are in non-multi point charges? What is the ratio of Anglo pastors to minority pastors serving multi-point charges?
17. What is the equitable salary level between minority pastors and Anglo pastors who have served the same number of years in pastoral ministry? What are the "promotion" rates?
18. What are the existing channels when problems arise? Do minority pastors know they exist? Have they used them?

RECOMMENDATIONS FOR THE STAFF-PARISH RELATIONS COMMITTEE

The responsibilities of the Staff-Parish Relations Committee are outlined in *The Book of Discipline*, ¶259. Paragraph 12 of the above-mentioned section says,

> To recommend to the church council, after consultation with the pastor, the professional and other staff positions (whether employee or contract) needed to carry out the work of the church or charge. The committee and the pastor shall recommend to the church council a written statement of policy and procedures regarding the process for hiring, contracting, evaluating, promoting, retiring, and dismissing staff personnel who are not subject to episcopal appointment as ordained clergy. Until such a policy has been adopted, the committee and the pastor shall have the authority to hire, contract, evaluate, promote, retire, and dismiss non-appointed personnel.

Summary of the Committee's Responsibilities and Pastor's Benefits:
• Total members of the committee should be 5-9 for the total charge.
• No staff or family member of the staff can be a member.
• A lay member to the annual conference is a member.
• Lay leader is an ex-officio, if not a delegate to Annual Conference.
• Term: Three years/Three year class.
• Retiring members cannot succeed themselves.
• No one can serve *forever!*

Meeting
• No secret meeting!
• The committee shall meet only with the knowledge of the pastor and/or the district superintendent.
• Multiple charges can meet independently when the pastor is present.

Duties
• Interpret the nurture and functions of the ministry.
• Consult with pastor and make appropriate recommendations to the charge conference.
• Enlist, interview, recommend candidates for ministry.

It is inappropriate for SPRC members to state or imply, "We hire and supervise you because we pay your salary!" The SPRC does not supervise the pastor. Like the SPRC, the pastor has a specific set of responsibilities in church, such as:

- is the administrator of the church.
- is the leader of worship and education ministries.
- conducts the Ministry of "Word, Sacrament, and Order."
- is a member of the conference and is sent to local church.
- maintains strict confidentiality.
- makes arrangements for pulpit supplies.

The Book of Discipline requires the SPRC to meet at least quarterly. The most important purpose of the committee or meeting is to keep the line of communication open and alive. The committee serves as a conduit for the flow of information from the congregation to the pastor, and from the pastor to the congregation in an atmosphere of strict confidentiality. In times of crisis, the committee serves as a liaison between congregation and pastor, and congregation and DS, who in turn passes on the information to the Bishop.

The primary responsibility of the committee is to interpret the nature and function of the local church's ministry. It empowers and enables the pastor to perform his or her duties and responsibilities as outlined in *The Book of Discipline*. The SPRC, in collaboration with other committees in the local church, writes job descriptions for the church's full-time and part-time staff and encourages young people to go into Christian ministry.

SPRC also encourages open itineracy, and cares about the spiritual development and renewal of the pastor and staff. During that process, the committee encourages the pastor and staff to sharpen their professional skills by doing continuing education and protecting the privacy and restfulness of the family. This committee also reviews, annually in accordance with the tool provided for by the conference, the effectiveness of the pastor and serves as a motivator.

The committee makes salary recommendations to the Finance Committee by following the guidelines established by the conference. Every SPRC is encouraged to give a minimum of a Cost Of Living Adjustment (COLA) to the pastor every year. Failure to do so will minimize the purchasing power of the salary the church offers its minister. In addition to a COLA, a salary raise, a merit increase, or special gifts may be offered.

This committee cannot meet without the knowledge of the pastor. Moreover, no secret meeting can be held! If the pastor is unavailable, then the district superintendent must be contacted.

Ways to Conduct Annual Performance Review

Pastors need to hear from their church members, committee members, and District Superintendent about their effectiveness in ministry and how to improve their gifts and graces. Their job performance needs to be evaluated in three major areas:

- Faithfulness to the call to ministry
- Competence and effectiveness
- Results and outcome

Of course, there are more roles the pastor plays than one can possibly imagine. Hence annual performance review must be based on sensitivity and fairness. It must also be based on the local church's goals and the pastor's shared vision. Avoid letting the review demoralize his or her ministry in the local church. Conduct the process with care and sensitivity, using it as a tool to motivate and encourage the pastor rather than as a put-down.

Start the review process with the goals set for the pastor and staff by the Charge Conference in compliance with *The Book of Discipline.* In preparation of the review process, try to study and understand the nature and function of pastoral ministry before you review the pastor's ministries in the local church. Prior to the meeting, try to read all the reports of the Church Council and committees presented to members throughout the year and then call for the meeting.

Bear in mind that the SPRC is not a supervisory committee of the pastor. The chair of the committee is not the supervisor of the pastor. The District Superintendent is the immediate supervisor of the pastor. The Bishop of the Annual Conference is the Chief Executive Officer of pastors and churches. The members of the SPRC and the pastor make up a covenantal team in the local church to create successful pastoral ministry.

If yours is a multi-point charge, establish an evaluation tool that the committee could use. Set up an evaluation system that gives the committee and the pastor continual feedback, rather than the end-of-the-year bombshell to which some pastors' appointments and salary increases are tied. The review must be based on the total ministries of the pastor, not a single or recent disastrous or damaging incident. Such incidents are often brought to the committee's attention by a disgruntled member or group from the church just prior to the annual review. Be wary when confronted with such a situation! Avoid including anything controversial in the review that has never been discussed before or never before been brought to the pastor's attention. All reviews, both the pastor's and the committee's, must be done in the context to improve and enhance the partnership ministry of the pastor and the church, not as a means of tearing down the pastor or the church at the end of the year.

If there is no review process currently in place or there is no missional goal for the local church, write one and share it with the members of the committee and the pastor for the following year's review process. Take the minister's skills, abilities, and availability, as well as the church's finances, church's membership composition, and so forth into consideration.

Remember, pastors are not superhuman! Hence, the pastor review must be based on the criteria established by *The Book of Discipline,* the conference, or the pastoral expectations set by the charge conference. These criteria are to be used by everyone on the committee. If the SPRC does not have a clear goal and the pastor is not given the appropriate guidance and support, the end of the year review will be a disaster.

Involve the whole committee in the evaluation process, not just the chair of the committee. Get a verbal response from each member of the committee in a regularly scheduled meeting, and put his or her responses in writing. Give the pastor an opportunity to respond.

Take appropriate measures to avoid inappropriate and hostile clouds that may be hanging over the pastor's ministry in the church. One of the important ways to avoid potential disaster is to intervene and involve the pastor and committee members when problems are noticed or brought to the committee's attention. Be mindful that the pastor and the members of the SPRC are a team. They are partners in the local church's ministry. Do not keep the pastor in the dark, and the pastor should not keep the SPRC in the dark.

Take every precaution to avoid demoralizing or placing roadblocks that obstruct the pastor's ministries. When concerns or problems arise, ask the person involved to offer possible solutions that may resolve the situation in an amiable way. Neither the committee nor the pastor can wave a magic wand and resolve a crisis situation.

Along with the review of the committee, there must be an opportunity for the pastor to respond in writing. A fair review cannot be one directional. It is a two-way street. In order to bring fairness and balance to the evaluatory system, the pastor should review the function of the committee and the ministries of the church.

Review both the mission of the church and the effectiveness of the minister. It is a covenantal evaluation. Write down all the valuable suggestions the SPRC has for the pastor to fulfill for the following year. Give generous compliments if the pastor has performed well or has a splendid job performance.

The review sheet must be signed by everyone in attendance at the review meeting, including the pastor, and then sent to the District Superintendent. Although the pastor may not agree with what is written, she or he must still sign it. This communicates that he or she has seen the written review.

Creating an Environment for the Review

The annual review must take place in an informal and non-threatening place and environment. This meeting is a closed meeting, where confidentiality is strictly maintained.

Avoid confrontational questions that might create a tense situation. When things get tense, language can become vulgar, attitudes become mean, and community and parochial loyalties supersede fairness and civility.

Ask the pastor to do self-evaluation beforehand and then ask him or her to share it with the committee. (See the sample self-evaluation form at the end of this section.) The self-evaluation may include the pastor's personal spiritual strengths, professional needs for development, growth and development, ministerial goals and aspirations, and joys or concerns in ministering with the members of the local congregation. This self-evaluation will help members of the SPRC understand what motivates and encourages the pastor to accomplish ministry tasks. It will also enable the members to truly review the pastor's relationship skills and performance in the local church. Ask the pastor to evaluate his or her performance in light of the following question: "What is God calling me to be and to do in this pastoral appointment?"

Use the response to this question as the beginning tool in evaluating the pastor's ministry. Encourage the pastor to share with the committee:

- the satisfying and fulfilling ministries of the church

- the fulfillment he or she derives from leadership functions of council and committees
- areas and ministries whose support and appreciation he or she has received
- disappointments and frustrations, if any
- failures and struggles, if any
- continuing education

Next, discuss the fundamentals of the pastor's commitment, the goals for pastor-church joint effort, and the values that the committee uses to measure the outcome. The following may help lead the discussion:

How does the joint effort contribute to the missional achievement of the local church? In other words, define the spiritual genetic code of the church and check to see if the ministries of the pastor and the church match. If they match, wonderful, if they do not, determine where, how, and why. Ask the church and its leadership to work together as a team more effectively.

All pastors are not alike. Evaluate the ministry performance using a range of methods—both qualitative and quantitative processes. There is no single methodology that expresses all issues that are important for evaluating a pastor's ministry in a local parish. Hence, be flexible in evaluatory method. Moreover, cabinet members and the Board of Ordained Ministry need to create a range of opportunities to establish metrics on an annual basis to review the pastor's performance. Getting the right results from a single piece of evaluatory paper is like reading a frozen thermometer. It may look right at the time, but it will lead to disastrous health very soon. Also, bear in mind that the pastor is on call twenty-four hours a day. In pastoral ministry, the boundaries between work and free time are blurred. This is why the committee needs to be sensitive in assessing the pastor's gifts and grace.

Consider and discuss the pastor and church as an entity and try every possible way to make it function as a successful team-ministry. After all, both the pastor and the congregation need to work together to give an effective witness as a church community. As an entity, the pastor and the church can strengthen relationship, foster collaboration, build strong mutual respect, and create a warm and understanding atmosphere for common ministry. Consequently, the SPRC review has to be objective, not subjective. It must be comprehensive, not particular. It should be based on the needs and concerns of the entire congregation, not just a few individuals or families.

Be sensitive to the pastor's cultural norms and values. The United Methodist Church's evaluation standard is mainly based on Anglo, middle-class culture and organizational setting. Unlike Anglo pastors, a vast majority of minority and ethnic-minority pastors' emotional energy and spiritual efforts are wasted on managing the mundane affairs of the church, as they have to constantly wrestle with racial and cultural prejudices. Hence, be open and sensitive to the pastor's needs, frustrations, and successes throughout the year. Put out fires as soon as they start, and wave the banner of appreciation whenever it is warranted.

An African proverb says: "When elephants fight, the grass suffers." Job performance evaluation is not a whip. If the pastor and the committee begin to argue and quarrel, soon it will spill over to the congregation, and the result will demoralize the church.

Do not merely close the review with a compliment. It should be supplemented with recognition and encouragement, frequently with a regular salary raise and other forms of open encouragement. The SPRC may tell the pastor he or she is important and doing a fine job, but the pastor believes that only when the members of the committee demonstrate that importance with openness and compensation. Hence, make the meeting a positive and supportive one.

Pastor-Congregation Ministry Review

The Book of Discipline, Part V, ¶114 says, "The mission of the church is to make disciples of Jesus Christ." The purpose of the Pastor-Parish Ministry Review is to promote dialogue in which participants may:

- assess the effectiveness of the ministry of the pastor/congregation team in the past year.
- identify focus areas for strengthening ministry in the coming year.
- plan for these focus areas to be addressed by pastor and committee.

SPRC's evaluation of the pastor must be focused on the following areas:

- Pastor-laity relationship
- Pastor's creative outreach and missional functions
- Pastor's leadership in the following areas:
    - Office Management—Administration
    - Finance—Fundraising
    - Church growth
    - Educational ministries
    - Other

Evaluate also the ministries of the church. After all, ministry is the teamwork of pastor and laity. Ask the pastor to evaluate the church in its missional context. Then the committee and the pastor evaluate the church in its missional context.

Evaluation-Conversation Guide

A) How effective are we as a congregation-pastor team in making disciples of Jesus Christ in the following ministries:

1. In our worship as a congregation? In being formed in the image of Christ as a community and as individuals?
2. In the ministry of Christian education for children, youth, and adults?
3. In reaching the unchurched? in welcoming visitors? in assisting new members?
4. In serving others beyond the local congregation as we help the world become more as God intends it to be?
5. In the stewardship of our time, talents, and money as a congregation? as individual members?

6. In the stewardship of our time, talents, and money as a committee? as a congregation? as individual members?

B) What spiritual gifts and skills of the pastor are most essential for the congregation's ministry in making disciples?

C) How has the pastor used his administrative, leadership, teaching, and preaching skills this past year?

D) What do we want the pastor to continue in his ministry and how does the SPRC intend to help the pastor fulfill that goal?

E) How does the pastor stay emotionally, physically, intellectually, and spiritually refreshed?

F) What do we want to improve as a congregational/committee team? Where does the pastor fit into this picture?

G) If the pastor's involvement in this improvement of team ministry requires more time in the focus areas, what are you willing for the pastor to spend less time doing?

H) What does this desired improvement demand of the laity?

I) Any other?

Signature of the Committee Members   Signature of the Pastor

Pastor's Evaluation of the Congregation

1. What have been the goals of the church for the year *(date)*?
2. How does the congregation care for the pastor?
3. In what areas does the congregation need to grow?
4. How does the congregation witness in bringing more people to Christ?
5. How does the physical property of the church witness to the people in the community?
6. How does the congregation practice spiritual discipline to keep the membership strong in Christian faith?
7. How does the pastor receive affirmation from the leadership of the congregation?
8. What does the pastor need from the local church to care for his or her needs?
9. How does the pastor care for herself or himself so as to maintain spiritual, social, and emotional wellness?

Questions for Discussion

1. Is the grading system accurate?
2. Is the year-end review objective and administered consistently?
3. Does it require the signatures of both parties: committee members and pastor?

Strengthening the Bond between SPRC and Pastor

The following recommendations came out of a consultation conducted by the General Board of Higher Education regarding minority pastors serving local churches.

- The Staff-Parish Relations Committee [SPRC] could set aside times to appreciate the pastor and his or her family. This could be done at Christmastime, when gifts are natural, as well as at vacation times.

- SPRC could plan welcome back home celebrations for returning pastors after Annual Conference.
- SPRC could take the lead in showing concern for the pastor and his or her family during times of crisis.
- SPRC could encourage the pastor and his or her family to build surrogate families or supportive networks within the local church, and it could help prepare the congregation for this possibility.
- SPRC could encourage the pastor and his or her family to fulfill the family's need for its own life, apart from the life of the church, and to create times where the family is "removed" from the pressures of church responsibilities. This also includes encouraging the pastor and his or her family to accept the nurturing that the SPRC can give.

As mentioned above, the support of the pastor should also extend to the pastor's entire family. Ask about personal experiences in previous local churches and communities, and then implement specific ways to show support for the entire family.

How to Welcome a New Pastor

After the appointment is made and the new pastor arrives, it is the SPRC's primary responsibility to welcome the pastor and introduce him or her to the members of the church (and community). Plan to welcome the pastor's entire family, specifically the spouse and children. Provide a tour of the church facilities and copies of worship bulletins, newsletters, and any other documents that might be helpful (such as charge conference reports, recent minutes of the committee and council, etc).

Make sure the salary, compensation package, and other benefits such as continuing education, and parsonage are adequate and comparable to that of other pastors and professionals in the community. A church that is unprepared to give a pay increase to its pastor is setting itself up for a less motivated pastor and a mediocre ministry. Bear in mind that a cost of living adjustment is not a salary raise, it simply helps the pastor maintain his or her lifestyle. Do not expect your pastor to tighten his or her belt because of your inability to provide an increase. Never try to find a spiritual interpretation for the refusal or failure to give the pastor a monetary increase or COLA.

United Methodist clergy are entitled to a minimum of four weeks of vacation and two weeks of continuing education. In addition to those six weeks there are other leaves and benefits (such as maternity/paternity leave, sick leave, and professional leave). Check with the District Superintendent or refer to *The Book of Discipline* for specific information.

Make sure all the records of the church (membership, constituents, shut-ins, Sunday school roll, minutes and reports of councils and conferences, attendance records, etc.) are in order and ready for the new pastor's use. If you have a pictorial directory of the church, give him or her a copy with the highlighted names of people who serve on different committees. Along with that, make available a brief history of the local church and community as well.

Remember to provide keys to all the doors and offices. Give the new pastor a brief orientation to the office, including information about software programs, e-mail address, phone and fax numbers of the church office, the name(s) of the staff and their working hours, the rules or guidelines of the usage of church facilities, and so forth. Also, provide a copy of the job description of the staff, both full-time and part-time. If you have an organist or pianist, give the pastor written or oral information about that person. That information should include the chain of command, compensation given, work schedule, compensation for special services, and so forth.

Try to meet the professional and living standard of the office and parsonage. Make sure all the appliances work in the parsonage and that they are safe to operate! Provide a map of the community, city, or town. If the pastor has small children, offer a list of available baby-sitters and their cost. Also, provide information about other churches in the community, the ecumenical programs, and the community events and programs. If possible, give information about local hospitals and health care providers available in the community.

After the family is settled into the parsonage, visit with the pastor and family at their convenience. Try to get to know the whole family. Set up an appointment with the whole family, and introduce the members of the Council and any other volunteer or appointed staff in the church.

When the pastor moves in, arrange for volunteers to receive the moving van. If possible, help the pastor's family arrange the furniture and unpack the boxes. Give a tour of the community and introduce the key people in town. In some small towns local people gather in a neighborhood restaurant at a certain time. Ask one of the church members to take the pastor and introduce him or her to the locals who gather there.

Respecting the Privacy of the Parsonage Family

Respect the privacy of the parsonage family. The church may own the parsonage, but that does not mean the Trustees and church members can walk into the parsonage anytime they wish. When the parsonage is occupied, refrain from going to the house without the parsonage family's permission. Moreover, the church has not hired two for one. Respect the pastor's spouse in his or her own right, not merely as the pastor's spouse. If the spouse has a profession or career, refrain from interfering. Avoid comparing the current minister's spouse with the former. Each person is unique.

It is very helpful to remember the pastor's birthday, wedding anniversary, and any other special events. Encourage the pastor to take a day off during the week, and ask the congregation to respect it.

Show Kindness to the Parsonage Family

Consider regularly extending acts of kindness to the pastor and his or her family. The following are suggestions that could be provided:

- An additional week of vacation
- A gift coupon for birthdays/anniversaries
- A special gift during Christmas
- Free baby-sitting occasionally
- Loan a car or offer a car repair
- Fruits/vegetables from the garden
- Help plant a garden

- Occasionally send a card of appreciation for the ministry
- Invite the pastor's family home or out for a special dinner
- Give a free movie ticket or gift coupons for pastor's children
- Offer to mow the lawn or shovel snow now and then

Show that you care about your pastor and the parsonage family.

CHAPTER 17

FOR MINORITY AND ETHNIC-MINORITY PASTORS

Successful ministry requires more than a desire to increase the membership, worship attendance, or revenue flow. It results from a combination of biblical knowledge, ministerial expertise, personal confidence, denominational loyalty, and deep commitment to Christ. All of which are developed through constant learning and conscious decisions.

Pastors are called to minister in that context, yet they need to minister with their own creative style. If you want to be taken seriously as a leader, you must let others know that you are sincere about ministry. Develop a fundamental knowledge of what will and what will not work based on experience, intuition, and assessing the church's needs. Always try to see the big picture.

Strive to achieve an understanding of the local congregation's perspective of ministry. For some pastors this is not an easy task since they are new to the culture, community, and church. Be mindful that each community, even each church, has a culture of its own. Get to know the visible and underlying components of this culture (i.e., what is said and unsaid). Everything else may fade away, but an abiding culture serves as the custodian of dreams for the church and for the members on whose faith and cooperation a pastor builds his or her ministry. It is an unchanging constant in the midst of a tornado of change, and it is something the church members depend on.

Cross-racial and cross-cultural appointments require minority and ethnic-minority pastors to disengage from their own cultural and social baggage willingly and deliberately in order to minister to the people they have been called to lead. After all, pastors are appointed to serve and minister effectively, not to convert or educate the parishioners to become like their pastors.

Try to understand mainstream American cultural assumptions and values. Translate the Word into the experience of the listeners and share the gospel in a contemporary format that is inclusive and redemptive. Such an exposition, as you are well aware, is called contextualizing the gospel.

Contextualization

Contextualization is to communicate the good news of Jesus Christ in word and deed and to find ways to engage in mission that gives meaning and purpose to the congregation you serve. By doing so you help the Christian faith make sense, meet people's yearning desires, and enlarge their vision of the world while remaining in their own communities.

We preach what we are and reproduce who we are. What we are dictates what we see, and who we are brings forth lasting fruits. Contextualization helps you maintain a fine balance between being an outsider and an insider: you totally identify with and are involved in the pains and needs of the congregation without losing your identity as a minority or ethnic-minority.

Theology is not easily transferable. Christian work, which is based on one's theological conviction, is deeply embedded in one's own everyday situation. In short, theology is contextual too, hence, the need to be multicontextual. It is good for Korean pastors to be with Korean pastors, or Indian pastors to be with Indian pastors. However, no one should be locked into only one ethnic or communal context. Try to be multicontextual, or in the Wesleyan tradition, try to be cosmo-contextual!

Contextualization is not all about the blind adoption of a new culture or merely living in a community, rather it refers to the transformation of one's ministry and mind toward the people one serves. It is like translating the gospel from one's culture to another culture in order to engage the listeners at the level of their deepest needs and greatest aspirations.

Most of the failures in cross-cultural and cross-racial ministry can be traced back to the failure of the contextualization of one's ministry in a local setting. These ministers found themselves branded as foreigners, outsiders, and cultural misfits. No culture is superior to another. Every culture has both good and bad elements. Culture is the water in which you catch fish. Yet, you have to catch them on their own terms, where they are, *not where we want them to be*.

The United Methodist Church exists to serve a larger reality than itself. As pastors you invite people to be a part of something far larger than what they can currently see—the kingdom of God. United Methodists have a culture of their own. It is called "connectionalism." Get to know it!

Striving Toward Faithfulness

The United Methodist Church is a global church. It is the second largest Protestant denomination in the U.S. Its polity and administration are vastly different from those of other denominations. Its infrastructure, expertise, and resources are designed to meet challenges, and to find and use opportunities to do mission work wherever and whenever the need arises. You are a small fish in a large pond! Hence, you must familiarize yourself with *The Book of Discipline*.

Understand the polity and doctrine of The United Methodist Church. Acquaint yourself with the *Rules of Order* of your Annual Conference and the structure of your conference, district, and local church. Read conference and denominational publications, and try to comprehend how the denomination functions, particularly the roles of the General, Jurisdictional, and Annual Conferences. Get to know the names of the general agencies and their functions. If your church observes special Sundays and supports conference and denominational advance specials, you will receive plenty of brochures and literature that provides a lot of relevant information. Read them. They are useful tools for effective ministry.

The Book of Discipline lists the functions and ministries of the general agencies. Additionally, several denominational magazines and other resources feature articles about the functions and ministries of these agencies. Read and use the information to promote mission and evangelism in the local church. Work hard to motivate the congregation to pay all advance specials and conference apportionments. It is an obligation on the part of every local church and pastor to pay their fair share of the support that sustains the ministries of The United Methodist Church.

Never condemn or criticize the denominational leadership or missional programs of the church in public. You and your congregation are part of the denominational structure. You, as a pastor, provide a face for the denomination, and you also gave an oath to the Bishop who appointed and ordained you that you would follow and uphold the polity of the denomination.

If you are unhappy about happenings in the conference or denomination, take appropriate legislative measures through the proper channels such as Annual Conference or General Conference legislation to change things. Avoid saying you are helpless or powerless to change or affect the policies of the denomination. You are a member of the Annual Conference, and one of the voting members that elects a clergy representative to the General Conference. Take your responsibilities seriously.

United Methodist Women

Take an active part in the programs of the United Methodist Women (UMW), and become familiar with its structure. Support your local UMW unit and encourage the women of your church and community to participate in the larger ministries of the organization. The UMW is singled out specifically here since research and survey data has indicated that several minority and ethnic-minority clergy have inadvertently committed administrative errors when working with the UMW.

As a pastor of the local church, you are an ex-officio member of the local UMW unit. The UMW, as a group, has a special function. It is not simply a women's fellowship. It is an organization and a vital mission unit, whose policy-making body consists of the elected directors of the Women's Division. Get to know it. Do not make assumptions about how the UMW functions. Certainly, do not tell them how they should function. They raise their own funds for United Methodist Women and administer the money on their own. There is no need to interfere in their mission or work. Further, all women in your local church are not members of UMW. Only those who pledge to follow the purpose of the UMW are members. In short, they are a membership organization.

United Methodist women are double givers. They not only give to the church, but also to the UMW. Consequently, they are doubly "connectional" people, one through the Annual Conference and one through their conference United Methodist Women. As an official United Methodist mission organization, they have their own by-laws and policies. The UMW is a part of the Women's Division of the General Board of Global Ministries. It has a unique and special function within the church and denomination. To learn more about the Women's Division, the UMW, or the general agencies of the denomination, visit their websites periodically for the most up-to-date information (http://gbgm-umc.org/umw).

CHAPTER 18

SUGGESTIONS FOR NEW PASTORS

B eing in a new parish is like settling down with that special someone. Now let the courtship begin—with the church!

The members of the local congregations want to know all about you. A good church won't and can't simply hand over the keys to church members' hearts. They have to consider many factors first. During the early part of the relationship you may be annoyed with the barrage of questions. But upholding your spiritual standards and administrative leadership not only ensures quality and excellence but also enables you to join the "family."

Success in church ministry depends upon providing what the parishioners are looking for and proving you have the qualities they need. They don't want someone who will come in and try to change everything about their ministry, because that produces chaos. The parishioners always look for someone who is open, willing, and committed to do ministry.

Hence you need to spell out your goals and share your visions for doing ministry with them. In other words, defining who you are is the first step in becoming a successful pastor. Right from the beginning, with the cooperation of the key leaders of the church, do the following:

Establish clear goals
  Get feedback
    Be willing to share
      Keep innovating

- Try to get to know as many families as possible in the first month. Memorize the names of adults and children. Call them by their first names.
- Maintain a journal and write down your impressions about the church and community.
- Read local newspapers, listen to local radio programs, and try to find out what is going on in the local community.
- Don't try to make immediate or major changes in administrative procedures or in the worship services. Go slow! However, display confidence and maturity.
- Have a clear mental picture of where you are going to take the congregation in coming months and years.
- Share your vision, plan, and goals in small groups and large groups, formally and informally, and ask for people's opinions and suggestions.

- Invite them to help realize the church's goals.
- Be realistic in setting goals and visions about the church's programs. Find out the church's wish list and engage people immediately.
- Be open to suggestions and new ideas.
- Be creative. Remember, creativity and activity are not the same.
- Build credibility as a caring, trusting, and approachable pastor.
- Expect opposition, doubts, and discouragement. Watch for potential grenades.
- Let the leaders of the congregation feel that they are part of the dream plan, and ask them to help you realize the dream. Encourage them to take ownership of the dreams you have for the church.
- Keep your eyes and ears open. Watch for contradictions and ambiguous statements.

Be aware of the pitfalls for new pastors: *Don't believe that every member of the church is pleased about your appointment.* You will be put to the test, so a wait-and-see attitude will prevail. You need to earn their confidence and trust. It may take a while. Be patient and sincere in your ministry. Note also that if you receive a *nice* appointment, your colleagues may be jealous. Just do your ministry and stay the course.

Regardless of your background, like in any other profession, you will be measured against your predecessor. As a minority and ethnic-minority pastor you have a big job ahead of you. If you are a minority or ethnic-minority woman pastor, your job may be like making a double-twist and perfect landing from a high bar! Be aware of your environment and do your best not to simply please the people around you, but to stay faithful to your call and succeed in ministry.

When you are being watched and under pressure, you will be tempted to make rapid changes. *Restraint* is the self-imposed motto. Avoid being bossy or authoritative. As part of their cultural backgrounds, some minority and ethnic-minority pastors are known for being *in charge.* However, being a pastor in the U.S. is much different from being a pastor in Africa, Asia, or Latin America. Know and identify the difference between authority and power. Pastors have authority but not unlimited power without the support of the congregation!

- Never forget to make a personal impact.
- Build confidence. Build a team.
- Move to the big picture. Balance it with details.
- Establish your relationship with SPRC to hire and retire.
- Loyalty is out of fashion. People move from denomination to denomination and church to church for a number of reasons. In times of confusion and personal challenge, don't be impulsive. Moderation is important.
- Avoid the urge to micromanage.
- Resist having an opinion on everything. Learn to say, "I don't know."
- React to the problem and not to the person.

Being faithful in ministry is something you are right now in the place where God has placed you. President Theodore Roosevelt said, "Do what you can, with what you have, where you are." It does not mean you have to travel to another place, have a bigger congregation, or have a financially secure church. You can be successful wherever you are.

Faithfulness is a process. It is not a list of things to be done or a list of goals to be checked off one after another. It is not arriving at a destination. It is a journey. It is a daily process. It is being in the ministry without quitting. It is knowing your call to ministry and growing to reach out to others. It is sowing seeds to bring comfort and healing to others.

Constantly revisit your dreams and update them. Take the emotional and spiritual temperature of the church periodically. Be a spiritual role model. By being spiritual, functional, and dedicated you can command love and respect from people. Be certain and confident in what you do. "For if the trumpet gives an uncertain sound, who shall prepare himself to the battle?" (1 Corinthians 14:8, KJV).

Be open to new ideas and suggestions. Promote collaboration. If you are thoroughly convinced of a program that might work for the church, share it with the leaders and ask them to help you try it. However, be cautious about any of your programs or visions that might display alienation of any individual or group that has had a prominent role in the ministries of the church in recent years.

Never give room to question your moral and spiritual integrity. Keep your word. Avoid doing anything questionable!

Sermon, Smile, and Shaking Hands

- Contextualize your sermons and Bible study discussions. Simply put, preach to the congregation's needs, not to yours.
- People go to church to worship, to fellowship, to be confirmed and reinforced in their faith. They look for a Word from the Lord being echoed and contextualized for their needs. Affirm them.
- Avoid making too many changes in the worship service.
- Change the order of service to suit your style ... but do not ignore the fact that the congregation has been accustomed to a particular mode of worship for a long time. Study the congregation, check with people, and make any necessary change to suit your style thoughtfully.
- Do ministry in partnership with the people in the congregation.
- Make disciples, not just nice people. Do not waste time merely making the church a warm, welcoming, and accepting place. Cultural engineering is not the end. Rather, people grow and deepen their commitment to Christ's ministry as a community.
- Exhibit confidence. Display enthusiasm, and strive to produce results in the church.
- Take time to prepare the bulletin. Let your and the church's image be projected through the design and the content of the bulletin.
- If you speak English as a second language, write in correct English. Do not hesitate to seek help from others. Your written communication goes a long

way. Avoid letting it be used as an evidence to show that you are an ineffective communicator.

All minority pastors have a disadvantage. They are not Anglo, and some don't speak Americanized English well. In addition, their food and cultural habits are different too. Do not allow mainstream culture to inhibit you. Bear in mind that the church is spiritual, so think, live, and act spiritually as an authentic pastor.

Work hard to avoid spelling and grammatical mistakes! Write your sermons and share your message unforced, unhyped, and unsanitized. Enable your listeners to face themselves and God so that their lives can be woven into the story of salvation.

Spend time in the office and read the files. Go through past meeting minutes and records. Learn where the congregation has been. Moreover, talk to the leaders of the church and try to find out the history and makeup of the church. Do not rely on only one source. Meet with people in hallways, fellowship halls, parking lots, coffee shops, and in every place possible. Attempt to learn about the local church and community in the first few weeks of your pastorate. After a few months, people will likely not tell you the story with unadulterated truth!

Be friendly. Smile! Be authentic and transparent.

Don't show favoritism.

Take every opportunity to listen: in the coffee shop, post office, public square, barbershop, grocery store, grain elevator, church gatherings—everywhere you go in the first few months observe, listen, and try to learn what is going on around you.

On the other hand, do not unnecessarily volunteer information about you or about your family. Let people ask questions about you. You do not have to respond to all questions. Anything too personal or prejudicial should never be answered. Be prudent. May all your conversations and small talks be seasoned with wisdom and sensibility.

Plan to stay in this church for the next five years or more, and act accordingly. Be careful in your speech and vigilant in all your actions. Avoid openly displaying your native country's flag or symbols that might give church members the impression that you are not one of them. Do not use "you Americans," "your country," or other terminology that might create a wedge between you and your parishioners. You are one of them. In the welfare of this country and the church you serve lies the welfare of your family and your ministry.

Be biblically knowledgeable, theologically informed, politically unbiased, ethically above reproach, administratively thorough, programmatically a team player.

"I am sustained by knowing that I am doing what is right."
Desmond Tutu

Be scrupulously honest with financial transactions. Accept no inappropriate financial responsibilities. Resist the urge to know who gives what to the church's treasury. It will enable you to treat all people equally. Do not allow room for suspicion or question concerning the vouchers you submit to the treasurer for reimbursement. Attach vouchers and receipts whenever possible, or provide written details about the expenses needing to be reimbursed.

Friendship

I will never forget Carl and Roberta. They were Anglo parishioners who were experiencing their first cross-racial pastoral appointment. They were faithful members of the church, where Carl was the part-time custodian and Roberta was the communion stewardess. We became acquainted over time and Carl, who enjoyed fishing, invited me to join him. I accepted his invitation, but I knew very little about deep-sea fishing. I knew even less about fishing for flounder from the shore. Carl was an experienced fisherman, and he was more than willing to teach me how to fish. He did this with patience and understanding. I am still not able to cast properly in spite of all his instructions.

One day Roberta told me that she wanted to share something with me. She told me that when she first found out that an African American minister had been appointed to the church she was greatly disturbed. She confessed that she had had a difficult time accepting the reality of a cross-racial pastoral appointment. Roberta told me this long after she had come to grips with her personal feelings. We had become good friends by the time she confided in me. If Carl had had any reservations about my appointment he never shared them with me. He would pick me up at 5:00 a.m. on our fishing days. Roberta always packed a big lunch for both of us. When we got to know each other as human beings and fellow Pilgrim Disciples, the walls of racism began to crumble. The conduit of Christian love could not be restrained or contained. We became friends in Jesus Christ and partners in ministry.

(ESL)

CHAPTER 19

FOR THE NEW PASTOR AND SPRC

A s soon as you assume your responsibilities in your new church, ask the church staff (you can also do it yourself) to notify the local newspapers, funeral directors, florists, and community organizations. Inform them that a new pastor has assumed responsibilities in the local church, and ask them to add your name to their database. Some local newspapers typically carry the names of local churches, their worship times, and the names of the pastors. Make sure your name is included and replaces the former pastor's. Also, remember to change the name on the outdoor sign, bulletins, newsletter, letterhead, and other places, if the former pastor's name appears on them.

As soon as you begin your pastoral ministry in a new church, if it is a multiple staff congregation, call a staff meeting. Ask them for help in locating important files, records, and documents in storage so that you can review them at your leisure.

If the church does not have a job description in place for the staff, create appropriate ones. If possible, include the staff in drawing up the job description, and provide a copy to the Administrative Council. Having current job descriptions for the staff is an important prerequisite to running the office efficiently. *The Book of Discipline* states that the pastor is the administrative officer of the church. This means that the SPRC and the pastor need to establish a clear chain of command for the staff.

No individual member of the church has authority over the church staff. (See the sample job descriptions in the Appendix). The pastor is the administrator and supervisor of the church staff. The chair of the SPRC does not have direct supervisory power over the staff. Allowing the SPRC chair or members to supervise the staff on a daily basis only creates administrative problems. Avoid them. The staff of the church is accountable to the entire SPRC, not just the chair of the committee.

If possible, create an employee handbook for the staff, which contains the work requirements or policies, policy on sexual harassment, and class I and class II violations which may result in involuntary termination or dismissal of the staff. Do not succumb to the excuses to avoid creating a manual often given in smaller churches such as, "Ours is a small church so we don't need them." Or, "We never had a problem before."

When a minority or ethnic-minority pastor is appointed to a local church, the rules of the game change. The work atmosphere varies. Be prepared! If the SPRC says that the church does not need the above-mentioned policies, follow through with your plans. Write the job description of the staff that was given to the staff orally by the SPRC, then at the next meeting read the description to them. Give the SPRC a copy for their records, and keep one in the church office file.

Hold regularly scheduled staff meetings, perhaps once a week or a couple of times a month. SPRC members may or may not attend such meetings. Have an annual Christmas party or staff appreciation party. The pastor should:

- Recommend to the SPRC, when appropriate, salary increase for the staff.
- Recommend giving at least a cost of living adjustment (COLA). Failure to give a COLA is tantamount to reducing the salary of the staff.
- Praise the staff when they perform, and institute ways to motivate them.
- Avoid feeling insecure when they receive more recognition or if they have more friends in the church than you do.
- If they refuse to take instructions from you or follow through on work you have given them to perform, do not take it lightly. Be persistent. Remind them, but after three warnings call for a SPRC meeting and take action.
- Never tolerate racial or sexual harassment in the church office.

Congregational Reservations

The year was 1971 when I was appointed as pastor of The Church Of The Good Shepherd in Willingboro, New Jersey. William Levitt & Sons had developed the modern day Willingboro. Initially in 1958 Levitt announced that he would not sell homes to African Americans. After a lawsuit was filed, he relinquished on his segregation policy and opened the community to African Americans. The Church Of The Good Shepherd was established by The Evangelical United Brethren Church and began to receive African American members as the community became more integrated. Although I was appointed to a congregation that was racially integrated, it became apparent that the congregation was in transition.

After I had been there for about a year, in a Sunday sermon, I shared with the congregation the three perceived strikes that were held against me at the time of my appointment as pastor. First, some folk felt that I was too young. I told them that time would take care of that concern. Second, some folk were concerned about the fact that I was not married. I told them that my recent marriage had eliminated that concern. Third, some folk were concerned about the fact that I am an African American. I told them that that reality would never change. We simply needed to get on with the work of ministry.

Over a period of five years we developed a good working relationship, as we learned to work together in harmony. Although the congregation was integrated, the Anglo majority culture was still dominant in the leadership and worship style of the congregation. We were learning what it means to be a multicultural congregation.

(ESL)

CHAPTER 20

FOR PASTORS FROM OTHER DENOMINATIONS AND CULTURES

The Appointment Process in The United Methodist Church

The United Methodist Church is not a congregationalist church, and does not follow the call process in making pastoral appointments. The Bishop of the Annual Conference, in consultation with members of the Cabinet and Staff-Parish Relations Committee, appoints a pastor to a pastoral charge. Hence you need to familiarize yourself with the appointment-making process and the duties and responsibilities of a United Methodist pastor as described in *The Book of Discipline*.

If you are a new pastor to the denomination, before being appointed to a local church, you will meet with the District Committee on Ministry, Conference Board of Ordained Ministry, and the members of the Cabinet. By the time your appointment is made, you will need to already have familiarized yourself with the denomination's structure and the appointment procedures by attending appropriate orientation and mentoring classes. Moreover, The United Methodist Church requires pastors new to the denomination to take courses on theology, doctrine, and polity before becoming candidates for ordained ministry. Requirements vary from conference to conference, but specific information is available from the District Superintendent or the Board of Ordained Ministry.

A few Annual Conferences require that ministerial candidates attend the School for License as a Local Pastor before being appointed to a church. At the school, candidates may be given inductive teaching about ministry in a local context. However, instruction varies from conference to conference.

The General Conference, the policy- and direction-setting body of the denomination, meets every four years. The policies and laws of the church are printed in *The Book of Discipline*. As a pastor, you will need a copy of *The Book of Discipline* and *The Book of Resolutions* to familiarize yourself with the church's laws and policies, as well as any revisions that are made by the General Conference. In addition, you will need a copy of your Annual Conference's *Rules of Order,* which is updated every year.

When in doubt about issues concerning the denomination and its polity, or the nature of the Annual Conference and its Rules of Order, contact your District Superintendent or the members of the Board of Ordained Ministry. If you have a mentor or a supporting cluster group, ask a colleague to help you understand the workings of the district and conference. Solicit the information you need, rather than assuming to know how The United Methodist Church functions.

Important Things to Remember

The following are things to remember as you go through the appointment process:

The United Methodist Church does not follow the *call* process like Lutherans, Presbyterians, Baptists, and other congregationalist churches. The United Methodist Church follows an appointment process, which involves the Bishop, Cabinet, and SPRC, who as a covenant team decide the appointment of a pastor to a local church. However, the bishop has the final authority to appoint or transfer a pastor in his or her conference. Hence, receive your appointments with joy and jubilation.

After your appointment is confirmed by the cabinet, your District Superintendent will take you to meet with members of the Staff or Pastor Parish Relations Committee (commonly known as SPRC or PPRC). This meeting allows both you and them to be introduced and get acquainted before your appointment is made publicly to the congregation and conference. Your meeting with the SPRC is *not* an interview. The local church does not have the authority to "interview" a pastor or take applications from any ministerial candidate. The Bishop asks the District Superintendent to clarify the appointment and introduce you to the SPRC before your appointment is publicly announced. That is why you (and sometimes your spouse) are taken to the local church.

Relax.

Go with poise

and confidence.

The SPRC cannot refuse your appointment on the basis of your race, age, gender, nationality, marital status, or physical condition. SPRC, on behalf of the local church, invites and welcomes the appointment made by the Bishop.

After meeting all the credential requirements, if the Bishop, members of the cabinet, and members of the Board of Ordained Ministry believe that you are able to perform your duties as a pastor effectively, you will be given an appointment in a local church.

Remember that ministry is conducted in the mainstream and by the missional expectation of the local church. You serve in the local church by appointment and invitation. You must prepare and equip yourself for effective ministry.

When you meet with the SPRC, it is normal to feel nervous. That kind of nervousness lies on both sides: yours as well as on the side of the SPRC. You are going to a new church and they are getting a new pastor. You are going to lose your friends and parishioners in your current charge and they are going to lose their pastor whom they have known for quite some time. They are new to you, just as you are new to them.

Both you and the congregation are vulnerable at this point. As a pastor, you need to be sensitive to the fears and apprehensions of the members of the church. They are losing their current pastor, who has shared the joys and sorrows of many in the church. They may not "be so sure" about their new pastor. Realize that the new church you are going to serve will go through a process of *grieving and gaining*. Be patient and sensitive during this time of transition.

New Pastor's Meeting with the SPRC

Be spiritually, mentally, and emotionally prepared before you leave your home to meet with the members of the SPRC. Preparation precedes success. Don't leave anything to chance.

- Dress professionally. The way you look is the first impression you give. You will never get a second chance to make a first impression.
- The way you speak says as much as the content of your speech.
- Your body language is an extension of your appearance and the words you use. Experts estimate that only 7 percent of our communication process is conveyed through the words we use. Another 38 percent depends on the tone of our voice, and 55 percent is through our body language.[1]
- Measure the tone of your voice and speak distinctly, logically, and confidently when you are asked to share a few words about yourself and your current ministry.
- Have a clear mental picture of what you are going to say and how you will speak to the group of leaders of your new church.
- Although your meeting with SPRC is not an interview per se, it is an important meeting that will determine your ministry in the church. *Do not take it lightly*. Mentally and emotionally, treat it as a formal interview. If there is a question and answer period, keep your answers short, informed, and thought-provoking. Avoid stuttering and stumbling.
- When you introduce yourself to the members of the SPRC, say your full name slowly and distinctly. If possible, prepare and distribute a printed sheet of paper with your full name, your spouse's and children's names, along with a summary of your resume or recent accomplishments. Ask them to look at your name, then read it for them. Enunciate clearly if you and your family have non-Western names. Some people do not readily know how to pronounce new names, especially if a name is unfamiliar to them. You need to help them correctly pronounce your name with confidence. Never apologize for your name, which may sound foreign to them.

- Tell them how you prefer to be addressed, such as Pastor, or Reverend, or by your first name. Consider being addressed by your first name. If you have earned a doctorate degree, ask people to address you as "Doctor" only in a formal situation, not otherwise.

During Your Time with the Members of the SPRC

When you meet with the SPRC, show confidence as well as care. Try to break the ice. Do not be afraid to use a bit of humor in your conversation with the members of the SPRC. Also, try to memorize the names of the members of the SPRC as they introduce themselves. This will allow you to use their names when responding to their friendly questions about you and your current ministry. They will be thrilled, we guarantee.

Try to establish a bonding relationship with the members of the SPRC with your genuineness, commitment, passion, and dedication from the beginning. If they ask about your current ministries and church experience show confidence in your ministerial abilities by your response. Avoid gloating about your academic credentials. Share your vision for the new church based upon the information the District Superintendent has already given you. Ask the members of the SPRC for their help in making that vision a reality.

Resist presenting yourself merely as a humble servant of the church. You are called to be a pastor and a spiritual leader. Therefore, exude confidence and leadership abilities. However, there is no need to portray yourself as an aggressive pastor either, who is determined to change everything they hold familiar and special.

You have the right to refuse to answer any question you feel is inappropriate. If the members of the SPRC persist, ask the District Superintendent to answer questions that are not comfortable for you to answer.

Do everything in your capacity to keep the meeting with the SPRC positive and upbeat. Never carry emotional baggage to the new church to show and tell, or to seek sympathy and take refuge behind.

Offer the members of the committee verbal assurance that you are open to suggestions and are willing to listen to new ways of doing ministry that will fit both of your styles. Let them know that you are a team player. If you want to be a successful pastor and a team player, you need to speak the language of your parishioners, wear their uniform, and organize yourself before going onto the field to play. In plain and simple language, be a part of the church community.

When the time comes to represent yourself, represent yourself fully. Never hide who you are. If you don't represent yourself, who else will?

Notes

1. Peter Kline and Bernard Saunders, *To a Learning Organization* (Arlington, Va.: Great Ocean Publishers, 1993), p. 191.

CHAPTER 21

PROVIDING LEADERSHIP WHEN THE FIRE IS RAGING!

(For Pastors)

Although it may be tough to follow in the heat of a crisis, Diogenes' dictum is key to maintaining an excellent relationship with the Bishop and District Superintendent. He writes, "A person should live with his/her superiors as one does with fire; not too close, lest that person burn; nor too far off, lest that person freeze." Rather than hide, pastors under fire should:

Maintain visibility.

Maintain credibility.

Maintain functionality.

During difficult times it is easy to lose sight of the broad view of ministry. Although cross-racial and cross-cultural ministry can be arduous and isolating, minority and ethnic-minority pastors must find ways to maintain their focus and stay true to their mission. The following are several helpful reminders:

Develop an individual style of ministry. Build and project a strong, confident image with colleagues and parishioners.

Identify hurdles and address them quickly.

Recognize and celebrate leadership differences. Too often minority and ethnic-minority pastors have the urge to be like everyone else.

Develop a unique style of ministry and leadership that is suitable for your local church.

Identify the visible and invisible internal barriers to effective ministry. Find ways to minimize them in order to do your work.

Avoid letting problems within the church fester. Try to defuse them immediately.

Be politically astute, knowing that each church has its own unique political environment.

Resist the urge to try to solve a church's historic problems. Although some members may expect you to do so, do not be naive!

Avoid going to the superintendent with local church problems unless absolutely necessary. Work to resolve problems within the church.

Take a few possible solutions to share with the District Superintendent if you must go to him or her about a problem.

Be candid with the superintendent about problems. Do not try to hide them since she or he will soon find out from your parishioners. Avoid placing your credibility on the line.

Admit mistakes when you make them. If it is a misunderstanding, work to resolve it. Never do anything foolhardy or unethical that may come back to haunt you. Remember that you will have to stand before the congregation to lead the worship service on the following Sunday.

Maintain an honest relationship with the District Superintendent and Bishop at all times. They will find the truth sooner or later, which will be detrimental to your ministry!

Avoid denigrating remarks about the District Superintendent or members of the cabinet. The District Superintendent represents the pastor to the cabinet and several committees that determine professional advancement.

Share dreams and aspirations with the Bishop and District Superintendent.

Avoid burning denominational bridges. Let troublesome relationships and bothersome experiences die on the vine.

Perform your job as a pastor well. Grow with the church.

Build the church community with your presence, giving, motivation, prayers, and preaching, rather than simply introducing new programs.

Be forward-looking and continually improving.

Be an explorer. Share the vision. Earn support. Accrue encouragement. Seek cooperation for your ideas before you launch them. Most of all learn to find a path of non-confrontation.

Remind the congregation of the mission and ministries of the denomination regularly. *The Book of Discipline* says in ¶201, "A local church ... exists for the maintenance of worship, the edification of believers, and the redemption of the world."

Use the church newsletter to spread the church's missional message. Remember the pen is mightier than the sword. Write pastoral messages, and use other sources of communication such as pastoral letters, member correspondences, and church bulletin boards to enhance the image of the church. Ask for editorial help from friends, family, or trusted laity.

Learn to communicate effectively. Ten percent of the world's economy is based on information and communication.

Communication is not a mere sharing of information. Communication is to convert information into knowledge, and knowledge into wisdom and wisdom into action. Authentic communication makes demands. It motivates the listeners to engage in action.

A Word of Caution to Ethnic-Minority Pastors

Some ethnic-minority pastors think of themselves as missionaries to Americans. This type of thinking is arrogant and illustrates a faulty understanding of church ministry. Such an approach to local church ministry alienates people in the pews.

One should know the difference between missionaries and pastors. *Missionaries* are invited guests who are constantly on the move. They seldom settle in one place. They go home or move to another place after a given task is completed. On the other hand, *pastoral ministry* is an ongoing, shepherding ministry that does not end.

Most ethnic-minority pastors are recent immigrants who have settled in the U.S. Many have no intention of returning to their birth country. As for their pastoral appointments, they are *sent* by the cabinet to serve a congregation that is already giving a mission witness in its local and larger community. Consequently, pastors who are sent to serve as worship and servant-leaders of a congregation are expected to know not only the lingo and language of the community, but also find creative ways to encourage the witnessing community already operating in a given neighborhood.

Language alters the perception of reality because people see themselves and their world through the words and the idioms they use. Language is the basis of thoughts and emotions, which in turn shape people's lives and behavior. In this aspect, some ethnic-minority pastors fall desperately short. They need direction. Seminary diplomas alone do not qualify them to be pastors, only the willing, loving hearts of parishioners can do that.

CHAPTER 22

SERVING SMALL OR RURAL CONGREGATIONS

Suggestions for Pastors

Indian theologian Raymundo Panikkar, who serves on the West Coast, points out that most people who write and talk about the world as a global village have neither been to, nor lived in a village. They imagine a village as a monolithic structure, which eliminates differences and is managed by a central authority. Only those who have lived in a village know that it is made up of a variety of subcommunities, such as race, ethnicity, caste, and class, each with its own distinctive style and shape yet still woven together into one community.

Our experiences when serving small and rural congregations have been positive; however, many non-Anglo pastors have not been so fortunate. Too often churches in small and rural communities are co-opted by secular forces. For example, economic, class, race, and even geographical and socioeconomic forces have a significant impact on these churches. In addition, resistance to cross-racial and cross-cultural appointments in these communities comes from congregations that have found safety and security in familiar ways of worship and traditional styles of leadership. In these instances, cross-racial and cross-cultural appointments appear threatening and frightening.

Some rural churches are fiercely territorial and do not think connectionally and missiologically about pastoral appointments. When this occurs, the missional concept of mutuality should be introduced with tenderness and biblical foundation and through education. Often rural congregations perceive these appointments as an infringement on their small town or way of life. As a result, before appointing minorities to a rural church, the cabinet needs to look for signs of openness and acceptance. Simply throwing a pastor into the fray will not work.

Strong family and communal ties are also characteristics of rural churches. In these communities, pastors are expected to participate in community events and support local organizations, some of which are controversial in nature. More often than not, decisions made by SPRCs and the church council are often saturated with the local community expectations, socio-cultural standards, and political norms. The boundary between the church and community is typically blurred.

The exercise of power also differs from community to community. Pastors from non-Anglo cultures may perceive the use of power differently, particularly in cultures that hold ministers in high esteem. In these cultures, pastors are endowed with enormous decision-making power. When pastors who have come from such cultures exercise their power in the same way as in their birth country in a smaller U. S. church, it is misconstrued as authoritative or autocratic.

Stress Factors: Loneliness and Family Life

Pastors and their families play key roles in the church. Unfortunately, they face expressed and unexpressed expectations from members of the congregation, and sometimes even the community. Most pastors recognize that their ministry will not be judged from preaching and teaching alone, but also by the examples they set individually and as a family. Such expectations can place great stress on them, as well as on their families.

Within one week, a pastor wears numerous hats that change at a dizzying speed: *preacher, teacher, administrator, counselor, trouble-shooter, mediator, writer, planner, Bible-study leader, supervisor, wedding/baptism/funeral officiant, fund-raiser, community organizer, mission coordinator, and so forth.* In each role the pastor is expected to be superior and well informed. Moreover, the pastor is expected to be always cheerful, giving, willing, and available, but never discouraged, depressed, cynical, or hurt. Such a dizzying role is overwhelming for a new pastor, particularly if he or she is from a different racial or cultural background.

Adapting to a new cultural and community environment results in some pastors' families feeling insecure and lonesome. They become uncertain about what to do or how to behave. This is a common occurrence among first-time appointees since they are least prepared to address this issue. Many minority and ethnic-minority pastors and families are lonely, primarily due to two reasons: *demographics* and *isolation*. They have been uprooted to a place that seems foreign and asked to live far away from urban areas and their cultural ethnic groups. Many do not have close friends. Although they need help dealing with this situation, many do not seek help. Ministerially and spiritually, they may be quite close to their parishioners, but socially and emotionally they are a great distance away from them.

Pastor's families may feel isolated when they are socially inadequate and self-conscious. Problems can also arise when they are unsure about the expectations of the pastor's family's role, particularly when following a long pastorate or when the spouse works outside of the home. The pressures to juggle church expectations and career development can be tremendous. There may also be pressure from juggling a family commitment or maintaining a united front while grieving the loss of familiar surroundings and people. Many spouses do not work outside the house and depend on a single income for the household.

Pastors are among the top 10 percent of the American population in terms of education, yet rank in the bottom third of occupations in terms of monetary compensation. This is a chronic anxiety and stress point for pastors and their families. Without an organized group to represent their needs, any mention of additional monetary compensation is likely to be misunderstood by parishioners, leaving the pastor and his or her family to suffer silently.

Unfortunately, sometimes non-Anglo pastors are excluded from church and community social gatherings. Ethnic women pastors and their spouses tell painful stories of such occurrences, and having to travel several hours during holidays and weekends just to be with friends and families to socialize and enjoy a relaxing time.

Too often pastors' spouses are expected to be role models of the church's membership. As the pastors' spouses they are expected to be active supporters of their spouses' ministry—a model spouse, a model parent, a model member, and a substitute counselor and Bible study leader—all without any concern for monetary compensation. Moreover, spouses are vulnerable to the success or failure of their partners' ministries in the church.

Church relocation or transfer affects every member of the pastor's household: spouses losing jobs, children changing schools and losing friends, and parents and children losing social support networks. Add to that the apprehension of moving to an unfamiliar community, and the attendant changes that affect minority and ethnic-minority families severely. It becomes apparent why stress and isolation are such prevalent factors.

Spouses are often expected to put the church's needs ahead of the family's needs, which in turn negatively impacts the pastors' families. Spouses can become torn between family needs and church needs. Often they live with the guilt of divided loyalty: *family or God; children or church;* or *personal time or church's service.* The stress and guilt are compounded for pastors who are singles and/or single parents. If the parsonage is located next to the church, the parsonage can become an extension of the church, rather than a private home. There is a lack of privacy as parishioners drop by at unexpected times.

Given the above, where does the pastor's spouse turn for help? Who is the pastor or counselor for the minister's spouse? Where does he or she go in times of need? These are tough questions, particularly if professional counseling is unaffordable given a limited income.

Clergy couples and single clergy have another set of issues. Clergy couples are in the public eye all the time, and are expected to be perfect role-model couples. This is also a stress producer. The boundary between their personal space and social space is routinely crossed. Spouses of pastors are a major source of emotional and economic support. Single clergy do not have this support, and they often must turn to extended families or ethnic groups for emotional and psychological help. Additionally, for many, their social life revolves around church programs and church members, offering few friends outside of the congregation.

Church ministry places tremendous emotional pressure and time demands on a pastor's family life, especially on evenings, weekends, and holidays. Late-night hospital calls and other emergencies pull pastors away from their families. There are always people with needs and crises, and pastor's families can feel neglected in the process.

Overcoming Stress and Loneliness

Listed below are helpful suggestions for pastors and their spouses in overcoming factors that lead to stress:

- Make a list of things that prevent you from making social contacts, and one by one work to reverse them.
- Love yourself as you are and, initially, seek those who like you as you are.

- Loneliness has its own advantages. It proves changes are needed. Changes, often, must begin within us. Ask yourself, "Am I doing all I can to establish lasting friendships with others?" Make the first move and mean what you say and do.
- Build relationships by being a genuine human being, and *then* a pastor. Share meals with parishioners occasionally, and sit with new people in social settings.
- Find a group with similar interests, and work to develop social skills and enjoy new friends.
- Read books on social skills and practice getting to know others and letting them know you. Avoid judging new acquaintances on the basis of past experiences.
- Watch local television stations, and attend events featuring local musicians. Listen to local radio stations and read community newspapers.
- Volunteer and connect with people in the community. For example, write a letter to the editor, voicing your opinion concerning a key issue.
- Cook a favorite food and eat with your family. Listen to favorite songs—in your native language. Take a walk as a family, or go to a local place of entertainment together. Unless an emergency situation warrants it, do not compromise your time with family members.
- Make an appointment to speak with a professional counselor or therapist when you feel extremely lonely or emotionally overwhelmed.

Suggestions to Cabinet and BOOM Members

Churches and conference leaders can help pastors and their families by making a pastoral counselor available. Moreover, encourage local churches to establish a healthy boundary between themselves and the pastor's family. Suggest that congregations allow spouses to choose where they can be a blessing to the church and the larger community.

Minority and ethnic-minority pastors and families are extremely sensitive to failure in ministry. If the situation arises, let them know that everyone fails from time to time, and not to let it affect their self-esteem or ability to function.

Too many families suffer from loneliness in silence. When they move into a new community, the pastor and family members may not adjust to their new home for weeks or months, despite the appearance they give. Ask church members to give the parsonage family time to make emotional and other adjustments.

Minority and ethnic-minority families are prone to difficulties after moving from a familiar surrounding to a starkly different community and culture, which has different ministerial expectations. Group counseling, cluster group therapy, and other support groups help a great deal.

As their families are adjusting to their new homes, pastors should be:

- Encouraged to set boundaries for themselves and their families. Also, they should be taught how to stand up for their rights. Asked to keep an open mind when meeting people and encouraged to show interest in them.

- Guided to take classes at local or community colleges that teach self-help, self-esteem and development, assertiveness, anger management, how to socialize, and how to become a positive thinker.

Church leadership is a series of spiritual ups and downs, emotional peaks and valleys. We need to strive for more peaks than valleys! Ministry is a calling. All pastors must be encouraged to keep running the race without quitting.

Serving as a Senior Pastor

For a minority minister, to serve as a senior pastor is antithetical to the normal role in cross-racial and cross-cultural appointments in some places. As a senior pastor, a minority pastor's authority may be challenged and questioned overtly and covertly, especially by subordinates. Hence, be prepared with the following:

- Prepare written job descriptions for all staff members.
- Promote teamwork.
- Create an environment of trust and love.
- Hold regularly scheduled staff meetings.
- Listen to staff suggestions.
- Keep written notes of what was discussed.
- Set priorities; then follow through on them.
- Coach and counsel staff about the congregation's ministries.
- Hold an orientation session for the staff about expectations (yours and the SPRC's) in order to fulfill the mission of the church.
- Delegate responsibilities.
- Avoid being a control-freak!
- Ask staff to keep you informed of church happenings and problems.
- Avoid being an authoritarian.
- Avoid competing with staff.
- Give staff latitude in decision-making.
- Hold staff accountable.
- Watch your manners, language, and body gestures.
- Dress professionally.
- Give continual feedback to staff, rather than waiting until the year-end review.

As the senior staffperson of the church, the pastors sometimes can feel alone and vulnerable. It is imperative to use professionalism, common sense, and good judgment at all times. When a staff member fails to fulfill his or her responsibilities, confront them. Written job descriptions are a great help in these situations. The job description should include a clear chain of command, with the senior pastor responsible for day-to-day administrative matters. If a staffperson is unhappy with your supervision, administration, and decision-making, he or she may take the matter to the SPRC for a grievance hearing. Guidance related to this grievance process should also be included in the job description.

The following are other suggestions for working with the church staff:

- Radiate dedication and high energy.
- Focus passionately on church's goals.
- Maintain an unyielding professional and personal integrity.
- Avoid losing your cool.
- Look for ways to grow and help your staff grow.
- Demonstrate infectious enthusiasm through your commitment and excellence.
- Motivate and energize your staff. Remind them that each of you works to promote the welfare of the church. Reward their efforts appropriately.
- Provide professional growth opportunity for each team member.
- Plan and strategize ways to succeed in ministry.
- Dream big dreams.
- Envision your future.
- Make sure that rhetoric matches reality.
- Manage the staff.
- Create a professional atmosphere, especially in a multiple staff church.
- Trust your staff.
- Encourage confidence in your leadership abilities. Whatever you do, do it thoroughly and remarkably.
- Offer clear instructions that are focused on the mission of the church.
- Use a consistent leadership style. Explain to the staff why you do what you do.
- Encourage a collegial style of teamwork.

If problems with the staff persist, talk with them individually, followed with a written correspondence. If the problem persists, refer the matter to the SPRC committee. Avoid creating a win-lose situation, which will serve to alienate the staff member's friends and family, who may also attend the church. Reading books concerning business correspondence and office management regularly helps sharpen communication skills. Books on communicating effectively with colleagues are particularly helpful. Below are additional ideas pastors will find useful:

- Occasionally, stop and listen to staff's joys and concerns. Always maintain a professional demeanor in your conversation with the staff.
- Never ask someone to do your personal work at the office or at home.
- Maintain a weekly, monthly, and yearly program calendar in the office and in your study.
- Delegate effectively to avoid overwork, while others have too little work.
- Ensure that everyone understands that everyone is a member of the same team.
- Use time at the office wisely. Plan and perform important tasks when staff members are present so that the task is shared and accomplished effectively.
- Take responsibility for the running of your office.

- Establish regular office hours.
- Have an answering machine or voice mail for messages when you are unavailable. Return calls promptly, preferably before the next business day ends.
- Answer business correspondences within a week.
- Keep your appointments. Be punctual, and when late, apologize.
- Learn appropriate ways to address people in writing and over the phone. Keep an English dictionary at the office. Typically, the back pages of the dictionary offer guidance on how to write and address dignitaries and religious leaders of various denominations.
- Maintain an inviting and clutter-free office.
- Keep a diary and time planner. Every morning, write a to-do list for the current day and the next day.
- Prioritize urgent tasks and act on them first.
- Write in your planner what you plan to do during the whole week every Monday morning. Revisit your planner and calendar everyday and regularly update it.
- Avoid over-scheduling your calendar.
- Hold counseling sessions at the office, *not* the parsonage. When counseling the opposite sex, let someone, especially the church secretary, know.
- Avoid leaving confidential notes or papers in plain sight at the end of the working day. Cleaning staff and others with access to your office may be tempted to read them.
- Maintain a good filing system. It is a must!
- Set a regular routine or pattern at the office. For instance, send information to the newspapers on Tuesday, prepare the bulletin on Thursday afternoon. Mail a copy of the bulletin to the liturgists or scripture-readers on Friday and so on.
- Avoid reading newspapers, magazines, or even devotional books while at the office. If you must, go to the church library or lounge.
- Do personal work such as balancing checkbooks and making personal phone calls at home, *not* at the office.
- Do not violate confidentiality agreements *ever*.
- Keep the church secretary informed of your whereabouts and how you can be reached during the day.
- Establish a strong professional bond with the church secretary and other staff. As members of the ministry team, they help make the programs of the church function efficiently.

CHAPTER 23

FOR ANGLO PASTORS ONLY

The following are suggestions for working with minority and ethnic-minority pastors and colleagues:

- Do not tolerate or accept the telling of racist jokes made by anyone. Insist they stop making racist remarks.
- Get to know minority and ethnic-minority pastors in your conference. *They do not all look alike!* Each has a name and an identity.
- Schedule an out-of-culture experience regularly.
- Read books on other cultures and people.
- Learn another language.
- Listen when minority and ethnic-minority pastors talk about their frustrations, pain, and feelings of hurt and rejection. Do not ignore them or assume it is their own making. When they talk about racism, prejudice, and the helplessness they experience in their congregations, do not undermine or deny their feelings.

> Womanist ethics and theology remind us that racism, sexism, and classism are not "out there"; they sink into consciousness, suffuse the concrete human-set up, penetrate all relations, and mediate meanings...the racist, the sexist, or the elitist fabricates and inhabits a world view so structured by racism, sexism, and classism that to behave otherwise is deemed abnormal. And hence the very humanity of all of us is disfigured. [1]

- Avoid cutting minority or ethnic-minority pastors off or labeling them as confrontational, abrasive, or problem immigrants when they share their feelings.
- Refuse to measure Christian ministry only in economic terms. Some believe if a Western missionary goes to the Global South it involves a sacrifice, whereas, if a person from the Global South comes to the Global North, it is a privilege. One may enjoy economic security, but what of emotional security and cultural safety?
- Do not believe that racism in the church or denomination is only a figment of people's imagination. Racism is a power arrangement. One cannot understand how people behave when they have power unless they have experienced it.

- Explore a minority person's experience. You may feel sorry about racism, minority bashing, and so forth but still feel the current system is fine. If so, you do not know the daily exclusions, hatred, abuse, and insults many minorities endure across the country.
- Manifestations of prejudice and oppression are on multiple levels. Hatred for the other is not limited to individuals who are mean and hurtful. Even policies, rules, legislations, and customs approved and enacted by institutions may give preferential treatment for some and marginalize others. Church is not exempt from such an act.
- Oppression is perpetuated by a socialization process. Since childhood we are systematically taught by media, parents, teachers, friends, neighbors, and relatives to inherit or accept an oppressive system. It takes a collective action and constant reminders to achieve the kind of society we envision and to transform the community. By simply going about your life you give assent to the status quo and approval to prevent change and transformation.
- Discrimination and exclusion of minorities and ethnic minorities do not have to be overt and open—just business as usual is enough. Hence you need to question the underlying assumption behind the policies, rules, and expectations.
- Resist asking a minority or ethnic-minority pastor to explain why a pastor from another minority or ethnic group behaves in a certain way.
- Remember that travel to an Asian, African, or South American country does not make someone an authority or interpreter of those cultures and people. Also, taking courses on multiculturalism, blacks, Asians, Hispanics, or other ethnic groups does not make someone able to explain or translate every ethnic group's behavior toward Anglos.
- Avoid telling a minority person that he or she is atypical or an exception to their ethnic group.
- Dispel false illusions about the mastery or understanding of all ethnics and minorities simply because of a close association with minority or ethnic-minority persons in your neighborhood, or parents of your children's classmates, or by eating frequently in ethnic restaurants.
- Admit that a minority is someone surrounded by a majority people who are different from him or her racially and culturally.
- Work to understand the difference between *similarity* and *sameness*. Appreciate and respect important differences. The experiences of different races are not interchangeable. Minorities and ethnic minorities have no control over their racial identity. Racism deprives them of control over who they really are. If you want to help minorities, do this:
  Forget that they are minorities.
  Remember that they are minorities.
  In other words, be normal!

Minority/Ethnic-Minority and Anglo Women
Women as a category and homosexuals as a category are examples of distinct minority categories in the U.S. However, many racial minorities do not wish to be combined

into a general category with other minority groups. Racial minorities need to be treated as a distinct category, if they wish, so that their issues are addressed fully. For example, a racial minority female falls under several layers of discrimination.

Anglo women and racial minorities may have much in common since both experience prejudice and discrimination. Race, however, is a major factor when it comes to discrimination. Post-colonial and post-modern theories offer plenty of reasons why racial minorities' experiences should *not* be compared with those of other minorities, such as Anglo women. There are fundamental and important differences between these two groups. First, racial minority men and women are valued less than Anglo females in Western society. Anglo women can claim all of the cultural and racial privileges of whiteness and maintain the normalcy that the broader culture offers. Consequently, they share in the power accruing to whiteness in ways minorities never can.

North American culture accepts Anglo, young, middle class, and heterosexual as norms. Racial minorities are seen as seeking special treatment if they request the same opportunities. The culture and its very discourse deem those who differ from the above presumed norm as wrong, lowly, and unskilled.

Power and Anglo Privilege

Although racism in the church systematically deprives minority and ethnic-minority pastors of their humanity by devaluing their individual and unique identities and talents, racism is only one of the multilayered systems of discrimination. Among the others are class, age, language, ethnicity, and country of origin. Usually one or two systems of discrimination are the primary source of the majority of problems. The common thread between the various layers is *power* and *control*. Power and control often determine ministerial, administrative, and appointment decisions.

"Power" and "whiteness" are synonymous in North American culture. "Power" and "non-white" are seen as mutually exclusive. While it is easy and comfortable for an Anglo to be both powerful and pastoral, it is much more difficult to pull off being a pastoral leader as a minority person.

When a visitor or salesperson comes to a church office, he or she invariably looks to the Anglo secretary or layperson and tries to transact business with that person. They are so familiar with seeing whites in positions of leadership or decision-making that they are blind to obvious disparities. Anglos are permitted a wide range of behavioral styles in North American society. Since minorities, especially ethnic-minority pastors, have not been well cross-culturally prepared as Anglos, they walk a thin tightrope. Majority and minority pastors often bring different approaches to looking at problems and opportunities to ministerial services. However, the more approaches available, the better the outcome for both church and pastor.

Many minorities and ethnic minorities have not mastered the subtleties of communicating with people of another race and culture. Too often they try to mimic Anglo males without understanding the basic differences between white and non-white culture. Sometimes the pastoral or ministerial approach used by minority and ethnic-minority pastors is too pietistic and moralistic, rather than contextual. This disconnect widens to catastrophic proportion in an unfriendly climate or intolerant atmosphere.

The highest priority at this point of the North American church's history is to *continue to move forward in its missional commitment,* and to *motivate the pastors serving in cross-racial and cross-cultural appointments.* By providing an environment where the great strengths and breadth of God's church can flourish, each pastor's and congregation's potential for service and ministry is enhanced. Moreover, they are better able to build a sense of teamwork and mutual endeavor across race, gender, cultural, and national boundaries.

All that minority and ethnic-minority pastors ask *from their Anglo colleagues in ministry is tolerance and acceptance, from the local churches cooperation and collaboration, from church leadership presence and encouragement, from the denomination belonging and meaning.* Sadly, all too often they find these things in short supply.

Notes

1. "Liberation, Gender, Race, and Class," in *Implications of Globalization,* p. 188.

Part III

What?
Resources for Ministry

Appendix

Sexual and Racial Harassment

Every pastor must familiarize him or herself with the issues of sexual and racial harassment. The first course of action is to read and understand the established policy of your conference on harassment. No one can hide behind cultural difference or linguistic ignorance when it comes to sexual harassment. The best way to prevent sexual harassment is to take appropriate measures. The following suggestions may help:

- Be mindful of your language and vocabulary as you speak to persons of the opposite sex.
- If your office is next door to your staff, let them know that they may enter at any time just by knocking.
- Establish a strict confidentiality policy in the church. The church staff may know who comes to meet with you and when. Sometimes they may even know the reason why. However, they must not share this information unless a crisis situation arises and the SPRC or DS makes an inquiry about it.
- Do not physically touch your staff unnecessarily. It is prudent to avoid touching your staff at all times while at the office.
- Avoid touching or hugging parishioners when you are alone in the office or in the building unless both parties feel extremely comfortable.
- Let the action to hug or embrace come from the other person, especially if the other person is of the opposite gender. Even then be professional. Do not initiate physical contact when you are alone.
- When you plan to meet with a person of opposite sex alone in your office or in the building, always let your spouse or the church staff know. Put the appointment on your calendar. Park your car outside the church building. Keep the curtains open, turn the lights on, and leave doors unlocked so that others may see you but not hear the conversation.
- Avoid being alone with a child or a teenager in the building or at the parsonage unless there is a specific professional reason known to the parents of the child and your staff/parishioners.
- If a teenager has to meet with you confidentially, inform your family or church staff or one or two church leaders that you are going to meet with that person. You do not have to let them know why.
- Avoid going to the rest room when kids are there. If you happen to go in, immediately turn around and walk out. It may sound like an over-reaction. Exercise caution and be prudent.

Guidelines for Sexual and Racial Harassment

The ... United Methodist Church believes that all persons are entitled to work, worship, and fellowship in church-related environments without any form of harassment. In keeping with the efforts to establish an environment in which the dignity and worth of all members of the church are respected, sexual and racial harassment of at the church are unacceptable and will not be tolerated. To this end, the church will neither condone nor tolerate harassment including derogatory remarks, racial or ethnic innuendos, sexual harassment, or any behavior that defames or intimidates anyone on church's premises.

The Committee advises staff members to monitor their speech and behavior in order to maintain appropriate professional and interpersonal relationships. When evidence of sexual or racial harassment is established, investigation and disciplinary action shall be taken, up to and including dismissal.

Staff members alleging harassment should report the occurrence to the Pastor or the Staff Parish Relations Committee, or the Administrative Council. All complaints will be dealt with in a fair and just manner.

In all cases, strict confidentiality will be maintained in order to protect the rights of the person bringing the complaint and the accused. Persons may serve as witnesses and every effort will be made to protect these persons against retaliation or intimidation. The church will comply fully with the law. No anonymous complaints will be entertained.

If someone who has brought a complaint is not satisfied with the results of the investigation and action taken by the Committee, that person may file a formal grievance with the District Superintendent.

Inclusiveness in The United Methodist Church
The Book of Discipline says in ¶117.

We recognize that God made all creation and saw that it was good. As diverse people of God who bring special gifts and evidences of God's grace to the unity of the Church and to society, we are called to be faithful to the example of Jesus' ministry to all persons.

Inclusiveness means openness, acceptance, and support that enables all persons to participate in the life of the Church, the community, and the world. Thus, inclusiveness denies every semblance of discrimination.

The mark of an inclusive society is one in which all persons are open, welcoming, fully accepting, and supporting of all persons, enabling them to participate fully in the life of the church, the community, and the world. A further mark of inclusiveness is the setting of church activities in facilities accessible to persons with disabilities.

In The United Methodist Church inclusiveness means the freedom for the total involvement of all persons who meet the requirements of The United Methodist *Book of Discipline* in the membership and leadership of the Church at any level and in every place.

Listen to the People and Your Heart

As a District Superintendent, listening to the Staff-Parish Relations Committee was a critical part of the process in making a new pastoral appointment. The purpose of this listening process is to enable the SPRC to share its deepest thoughts/concerns about a new appointment. A critical issue is the matter of the kind of pastoral leadership that is needed in a congregation at a particular time. Does the pastoral leader possess the necessary gifts and grace that is needed by the congregation? The role of the District Superintendent is to listen carefully to the SPRC; then he or she communicates to the Cabinet what she or he has heard with candidness and integrity. The DS's personal reservations, latent prejudices and fears must be set aside.

I remember meeting with a SPRC and listening to their conversation regarding their description of the pastoral leadership skills that were needed at that time. After reflecting on their descriptive analysis, I reported to the Cabinet. During the Cabinet discussion pertaining to our selection of a new pastor, I suggested the name of a pastor who fit well the leadership needs description shared by the SPRC. The Bishop decided to appoint this person. When I introduced the new pastor to the SPRC, there was some reservation about the fact that the new pastor would be a woman. After much discussion with the SPRC about this concern and other issues, the Cabinet determined to proceed with the appointment. This female pastor began to give extraordinary leadership to the congregation, and the congregation began to grow in spirit and in membership. It was a matter of matching the gifts and grace of a particular pastor with a specific congregation. In this instance the minister was female and Anglo, and it was an Anglo congregation.

I have learned the importance of diligently seeking to match a pastor's gifts and grace with the right congregation after the Cabinet listens effectively to what the SPRC is saying. When I recommended a woman to be the next pastor, I was listening to the SPRC and I was listening to my heart. My heart was telling me to do the right thing, because there was a match. The Spirit was right and my spirit is at peace. This is an important principle when confronting the *isms* in our society, especially racism.

Resources for SPRC, Pastors, and Local Church Trustees

According to research and conversations with both pastors and laity, the root cause of the administrative problems several minority and ethnic-minority pastors face in local churches can be traced back to the lack of job descriptions or written guidelines provided by the SPRC and Cabinet in managing the local church staff. If job descriptions for the staff and guidelines for the usage of the church's facilities had been clearly spelled out, perhaps a lot of headaches could have been avoided. Both small and large churches have fallen short in this area.

The following sample forms are provided to enable pastors, SPRC, Trustees, and Cabinet members to design job descriptions for staff and guidelines for the usage of facilities that are suitable for local churches.

SAMPLE FORMS AND POLICY GUIDELINES[1]
(For SPRC)

Updated On: _____

Staff Vital Information
Confidential

Full Name of the Staff:

Date Appointed/Hired:

Social Security Number:

Pension Plan Participant Number:

Health Insurance Number:

Birth Date:

Spouse's Name:

Dependents, if any:

Home Address:

Home Phone:

Emergency Telephone Number:

Current Salary:

Other Benefits:
> Pension Contribution—Personal
> Pension Contribution—Church's Share
> Social Security—Church's Share
> Health Insurance
> Housing

Other Information:

Sample Job Description for Youth Director

Name:

Address:

Job Title:

    (Full-time/Part-time)

Date Hired/Appointed:

Salary:

Total Number of Work Hours:

Special Conditions:

JOB-RELATED BENEFITS:

    Holidays

    Sick Days

    Continuing Education

    Pension

    Health Insurance

    Other

SUPERVISOR:

REPORTS TO:

DUTIES AND RESPONSIBILITIES:

(Example: As Youth Coordinator of the . . . UMC, the staff member has a dual responsibility of serving both as Staff Assistant for Education and Youth Director of Outreach Ministries.)

The responsibilities include to:

- *serve on the Education Committee as staff contact for Christian Education and carry on the responsibilities as outlined in the <u>Guidelines</u> of the Education Committee.*
- *sesign, plan, and implement educational opportunities to expand concepts of mission within the church and its school.*
- *strengthen the current Sunday school ministries in cooperation with the Sunday School Superintendent.*
- *coordinate the educational aspects of the church's VBS, Sunday school, and other instructional programs.*
- *plan and execute teacher training events at least once a year.*
- *scoordinate all Junior and Senior High Youth activities.*
- *serve as a mentor and guide to the children and youth group leaders and plan for summer camps, choir trips, Disciple Bible Study, etc.*
- *resource the classrooms, motivate and train the volunteer staff for all educational programs.*
- *provide program information about education nd evangelistic ministries to the Pastor nd church office to set dates and plan the program calendar for the whole year.*

- *serve as the steering leader for youth evangelism.*
- *if need be, preach sermons when the pastor is on leave. Make hospital calls on emergency situations.*
- *coordinate and do children's moments and Junior Church for Sunday morning.*
- *call on new families who have moved into town. Pay more attention in calling on families who visit our church services on Sunday morning, meet them in their homes within forty-eight hours and invite them to church and Sunday school.*
- *serve as ex-officio member on Education, Outreach, and Evangelism committees.*

SPECIAL WORKING CONDITIONS:

Working during some holidays, evenings, and weekends may be frequent. Travel out of town to attend youth camps or workshops may be necessary.

Regular office hours should be maintained in order for the church members to contact the Youth Minister. Total number of hours to be put in per week is 20.

This position requires contact on a regular basis with individuals and groups which are not part of the ... United Methodist Church's membership. This work has an integrity which the church respects as a part of its ministry. In all areas of the church's ministry, confidentiality in relationships must be respected.

QUALIFICATIONS:

Membership in The United Methodist Church is required.
Lay Speaker's Training desired.
Extensive communication skills needed, both written and verbal.
Professional ability to relate to youth.
Genuine human interest to interpret the concerns of the youth to Pastor and/or appropriate committees.
Ability to work with a variety of persons, including volunteers.

Sample Job Description for Church Secretary

Name:

Address:

Job Title: **Church Secretary**

Date Hired:

Position: Full-time/Part-time

Salary:

Mandatory Retirement Age (as set by SPRC):

Special Conditions: *Appointment is Voted Annually SPRC*
JOB RELATED BENEFITS:

> Vacation: *First Year: Prorated one week*
> > *2 to 10 years, 2 weeks*
> > *11 to 16 years, 2 weeks and 3 days*
> > *7 to 27 years, 3 weeks*
> > *28 and above, 4 weeks*
>
> Number of days for sick leave:
> Number of personal days:
> Pension Benefits:
> Health Insurance Benefits:

SUPERVISOR: *Pastor of the Church*
ACCOUNTABLE TO: *Pastor and Staff-Parish Relations Committee of . . . UMC*
DUTIES AND RESPONSIBILITIES:
(Example: Serve as secretary of the church and have general office responsibility for the work of the congregation in keeping with its missional purpose.)

The Church Office hours:
> Monday-Friday
> *8:30 A.M.-4:30 P.M.*
> *Lunch Break: 12:15 P.M.-1.00 P.M.*
> *(Office holidays are set by SPRC)*

Prepare Sunday Bulletins. Check calendar to make sure that no announcements have been missed. Double check page numbers with hymnal. Mail bulletins to the liturgists, greeters, and ushers, and to the radio station and newspaper.

On Thursday afternoon or Friday morning call and remind the nursery staff, van drivers, and greeters.

Prepare monthly Newsletter with guidance from the Pastor. Coordinate the church program calendar.

Maintain Church Membership Records up-to-date by noting changes of name, status (deaths, baptisms, transfers, etc.)

Do all office correspondence: Type letters, reports, committee minutes, and all work related to church, district, and conference. Pick up and sort out mail to appropriate committees.

Provide coordination and offer services related to committee meetings and mailings.

File documents/correspondences in appropriate files. Receive bills/vouchers for the budget-approved items, double check them and provide assistance to the Treasurer of the church to make the payments on time. All payment vouchers should be checked and verified twice for the work performed or merchandise ordered before placing them on Pastor's desk for counter signature.

Help the Treasurer in completing the required federal and state tax payments and reports, and mail them on time.

Answer all incoming church calls with professional courtesy and return all calls left on the answering machine the next working day.

Maintain an up-to-date church program calendar and record it on the yearly wall calendar for committees to plan for their meetings and programs.

Ability to articulate the policy and position of the ... United Methodist Church and provide guidance in general planning and coordination of the church's total program, including implementation of the church's missional policies as established by the Church/Charge Conference.

In consultation with the Pastor and Chairpersons, call and remind the members of the scheduled committee meetings. Only those whom cannot be reached by phone should get a card.

Provide the Computer Operator with all financial information whenever necessary for the staff to prepare the financial statement.

Other duties as assigned by the Pastor and/or SPRC.

WORKING CONDITIONS:
Regular office hours should be strictly maintained.
Professional atmosphere should be kept at all times limiting personal and social contacts with friends and family members so that matters of church can be maintained.
Christian commitment to work with volunteers. Extensive communication skills needed, both written and verbal. Professional ability to relate to adults and parents. General administrative skills.
This position requires contact on a regular basis with individuals and groups who are part of the ... United Methodist Church's membership. This work has an integrity which the church respects as a part of its vital ministries. In all areas of the church's ministry, confidentiality in relationships must be respected.

QUALIFICATIONS:
> *Membership in The United Methodist Church is desired.*
> *Commitment to work with volunteers.*
> *Good verbal and writing skills.*
> *Computer skill is a must.*

Sample Job Description for Church Custodian

Name:

Address:

Title: **Church Custodian**

Date Hired:

Salary:

Position: Part-time/Full-time

 Special Conditions: *Voted Annually by SPRC*

Job Related Benefits:

All applicable office holidays.

SUPERVISOR: *Pastor of the Church or Church Secretary when Pastor is unavailable*

ACCOUNTABLE TO:

Pastor, Church Secretary and Pastor-Parish Relations Committee of ... UMC with yearly evaluation.

DUTIES AND RESPONSIBILITIES:

- *Work includes custody, care, and cleaning of building and grounds.*
- *Prepare the sanctuary and set up the altar according to the UMC program calendar and church seasons. Check the pews for supplies and refill them. Check all lights and replace bulbs.*
- *Inspect the building once a week and report to Pastor about abuse of building, damage caused by natural elements, and other wear and tear.*
- *Prepare the sanctuary, halls, and appropriate rooms for weddings and celebrations by members and nonmembers. An honorarium is set for help with weddings.*
- *Clean all rooms once every week and take garbage out. Check the restrooms thoroughly twice a week and make sure they have enough supplies. Vacuum all carpeted areas once a week. Vacuum the carpet in the foyer every day when the custodians come to work.*
- *Wash windows in office, ground level windows, and doors in the building periodically.*
- *Check the kitchens everyday when the custodians come to work and make sure no food particles are left on the floor. Vacuum and mop the floors thoroughly. No food garbage should be left in the kitchen for more than a night during the week.*
- *Special attention should be paid to stairs, elevators, and hallways all year long. They should be clean and slippery free.*
- *Check with office calendar and minister for all regular and special meetings of the congregations.*
- *Store flammable cleaning agents, paints, polishes, etc., in a safe place.*
- *An inventory of hazardous materials must be maintained. All containers must be labeled with the identity of the hazardous material contained and the appropriate hazardous warnings. They should be kept out of reach of children and stored in the supply room.*
- *Make sure enough fire extinguishers are kept in each level and one in each kitchen, and they are serviced regularly.*

- *Store valuables and supplies in appropriate storage areas/closets. Before leaving the building make sure all the doors and windows are secured.*
- *Make sure the emergency telephone numbers are taped near the telephone equipment for all to see.*

QUALIFICATIONS:

Christian commitment to work with volunteers. Ability to relate to members and chairpersons of committees. Flexibility to work during weekends to prepare the building/sanctuary for worship service after weddings, funerals, etc.

This position requires contact on a regular basis with individuals and groups that are not part of the . . . United Methodist Church's membership. This work has an integrity that the church respects as a part of its ministries. In all areas of the church's ministry, confidentiality in relationships must be respected.

Sample Job Description for Church Organist

Name:
Address:
Title: **Church Organist**
Date Hired:
Position: Part-time/Full-time
Salary:

$_____ per Sunday morning worship service
$_____ per rehearsal
$_____ per Special Service and/or Rehearsal
$_____ per Wedding
$_____ per Funeral

The Organist will let the church office know the fee he/she charges for marriages (including rehearsal) and funerals. The church office will pass the information to the families. The Organist will make direct arrangements with the marrying couple or Funeral Director about the method of payment.

Special Conditions: *Voted Annually by SPRC*
SUPERVISORS: *Music Director, Pastor*
ACCOUNTABLE TO: *Pastor and Staff-Parish Relations Committee of . . . UMC with yearly evaluation.*
DUTIES AND RESPONSIBILITIES:

The Organist will perform the following duties under the direction of the Music Director.
- *Play organ or piano for Sunday worship services.*
- *Rehearse with the choir members on Wednesday evenings and help the Music Director to enable the choir perform special music on Sunday mornings.*
- *Play for Special Worship Services such as (Maundy Thursday/Good Friday/Christmas Candlelight Service)*
- *Play for children/youth and adults when they perform special programs for the church and be available for rehearsal/practice as the Music Director determines.*
- *Play music for the prelude/postlude, offering.*

Special Working Conditions:
- *Sunday morning work is primary.*
- *This position requires contact on a regular basis with individuals and groups which are part of the ... United Methodist Church's membership. This work has an integrity which the church respects as a part of its ministries. In all areas of the church's music ministry, cooperation with the Choir Director and choir members is essential.*

If Appointed:
All appointments in the ... United Methodist Church are renewed annually in the month of July as the new Annual Conference year begins.

Sample Use of Church Building Policy

Method of Adoption and Agreement:
Upon adoption by the . . . UMC Board of Trustees and Church Council, this Church Use Policy and its companion Church Wedding Use Policy will supersede all previous policies and procedures. It may be amended by majority vote of the Trustees and/or Church Council.

Weddings:
Please see the current copy of our Church Wedding use Policy sheet.

General Philosophy:
The . . . United Methodist Church belongs to God and exists for the conduct of worship and due administration of God's Word and Sacraments, the maintenance of Christian fellowship and discipline, the edification of believers, and the conversion of the world.

When not in use for these purposes, it may be rented by members of . . . United Methodist Church, outside individuals, groups, and organizations, provided they do not hamper the church's ministry or conflict with The Book of Discipline of the United Methodist Church.

Priority of Use:
This building will be rented to individuals and small or large groups which do not conflict with our General Philosophy on a first-come, first-served basis—as determined by when those events are listed on the Church Calendar maintained at the office.

However, the programs of the church shall take priority over all the others.

Every effort will be taken to communicate to the renters of the facilities before a church program is scheduled. However, if emergency services, church/denominational meetings and conferences, or spiritual programs are organized by the church, all the scheduled programs will be provided either an alternate room(s) or asked to reschedule their meetings with or without prior notice.

Every group that uses the facilities shall enter into a contractual agreement with the Trustees of the church.

The service charge of the facilities shall be negotiated every year.

Long-time users will be given discount, up to a maximum of 50 percent of the rental fee. No one shall get more than 50 percent discount as the rental cost has been kept extremely low to accommodate individuals and groups from all economic backgrounds.

Any reduction in cost of rent as outlined above will adversely affect the finances of the church in maintaining its facilities.

The groups that use the church facilities are encouraged to make donations to pay for the utilities of the building.

All contracts are established for only one year at a time (unless otherwise stated) as The Book of Discipline of the United Methodist Church mandates. The current committee's decision should not bind the future committee members' innovative plans to use the facilities for the furtherance and extension of the ministries of the church.

Every year the renters will be asked to meet with the Board of Trustees at a regularly scheduled or called for meeting to renew the contract for the following year. The contract should contain the following information:

> *The name of the user*
> *The cost of service charge*
> *Compliant Policy*
> *Method of Payment*
> *Other papers such as insurance, etc.*
> *Any other documents the Board of Trustees requires*
> *Signed legal agreement*

Unless otherwise stated, usage of other than the assigned room or hall will be deemed a violation of the contract.

The church and/or the Board of Trustees hold the right to terminate a contract if the renters misuse the facilities or violate the agreement.

No one can assume that the church will rent its facilities forever. All rental agreements are based on availability, fair rental value, and subject to the mission statement of the church as defined by the church.

Failure to renew the rental contract with the Board of Trustees before the beginning of a new year will result in renting the facilities to others in line.

Please see the Pastor or Church Secretary or Chair of the Trustees for more details.

Storage Policy:
No one who rents the church facilities can store any personal or organizational items. Violators will be charged for the storage and the items will be removed and discarded without notice.

The Board of Trustees and the church will not be held responsible for any unauthorized storage.

Lost Items:
Neither the church nor the Board of Trustees is responsible for any lost item.

Setting Up the Night Before:
Groups or individuals may wish to set up for major dinners and programs the night before they are to occur. This will be permitted only if it does not interfere with events previously

scheduled and only with the understanding that a funeral dinner may have to be scheduled at the last minute. Such things cannot be planned ahead of time.

Routine Clean-up:

All groups and individuals using the building are expected to clean up after themselves and to put the hall(s) and room(s) back exactly as they found them. This includes washing dishes and silverware that have been used, cleaning up things that have been spilled or tracked in, and placing all tables and chairs back exactly as they were found.

It also includes making sure all lights have been turned off (including restrooms), all toilets have been flushed, all paper has been picked up, and all windows have been closed. Unless previous arrangement has been made with the Pastor, Church Secretary, or Chair of the Trustees, this also includes making sure all doors have been locked.

All groups and individuals using the church facilities will be billed and expected to pay for any breakage or excess clean-up that needs to be done. In such cases, deposits will not be refunded and future use of the facilities will be denied to them.

Free Usage:

Upon the annual recommendation of the Pastor or the Trustees or the Church Council, certain civic or not-for-profit organizations will be granted permission to use the facilities free of charge for a maximum of two times a year.

All contributions are welcome from them, of course, and the donations will be used for church upkeep, utilities, and improvement by the Trustees.

Borrowing Church Equipment:

Except tables and chairs, no electronic equipment, musical instruments, or any other church property can be rented from the church. Neither should they be loaned or removed from the church premises.

Use of the Sanctuary:

The Sanctuary shall not be used for any social or community events.

Under no circumstances shall there be food or drink (other than the Holy Communion) taken to the sanctuary. The furniture, musical instruments, vestments, or anything placed in the sanctuary shall not be moved or removed from their location without prior permission from the Pastor and/or Chair of the Trustees.

Use of Alcohol, Tobacco, and Illegal Drugs:

Smoking is not permitted anywhere in the Church Building, including restrooms. The use of alcohol and illegal drugs is not permitted in the building or anywhere on church grounds. Anyone abusing this rule will be instructed to leave the church premises and the usage of the facilities will be revoked forthwith.

No fees or deposit will be returned. Serious offenders will be prosecuted.

Multiple Usage:
It is often possible for more than one meeting or event to be going on at a given time. Consequently, scheduling part of the church for one meeting does not guarantee that another part of the church will not be used by another group.

Fees:
<u>*The following fees must be paid in advance during the time of reservation. The availability of*</u> <u>*the facilities is not guaranteed until the money is brought to the church office.*</u>

The fees must accompany Building Use Request Form in the form of a check made payable to ... United Methodist Church. If building use is denied, the money will be refunded. Filling in the application form does not guarantee the approval of the usage of the facilities. The Trustees of the church are solely responsible for the approval and denial of the request.

The fees for the use of facilities both by members and non-members are as follows:

Refundable Deposits:

Sanctuary alone (non-members)	$
Fellowship Hall	$
Fellowship Hall with Kitchen privileges*	$
Room	$
Tables (each)	$
Chairs (up to ten)	$

*Kitchen privileges: Usage of refrigerator, stove, sinks for food preparation and serving. If food is being served, fee for kitchen privileges will be included.

(For regularly scheduled events and multiple usage of the facilities, discounts will be considered by the Trustees.)

Contingencies and Variances:
All rental contracts/agreements are effective only for a year, from January through December, unless otherwise stated.

During the Trustees and/or Church Council meetings in December, all the rental requests will be discussed and reviewed for renewal or termination.

In accordance with The Book of Discipline of The United Methodist Church, no committee can enter into a permanent contractual agreement with the renters and hence the renters will be notified about the established policy of the church by the Board of Trustees during the time of the renewal of the contract.

Because no policy can cover every contingency, it is possible to apply for a variance to one or more of the above rules. An appeal for variance must be submitted in person or writing to the Trustees or Church Council in enough time for the committee(s) to deal with them at their regularly scheduled meeting.

A custodial fee of $50.00 is also involved for the use of the facilities on top of the above charges depending upon the area of the use.

(Revised Date_____)

Sample Information Sheet for Church Weddings

The United Methodist Church considers the Wedding Ceremony as one of the most sacred events in human life. From time immemorial, the Church has stressed the importance and sacredness of this rite.

Our beautiful sanctuary, when used in the spirit of true worship, makes possible a reverent and sacred wedding ceremony that will always be remembered not only by the bride and groom but also by their friends and families. To that end, we call attention to the following regulations:

1. It is assumed that the Pastor of the church will be consulted for all weddings to take place in this church.

To avoid disappointment, confer with the Pastor, get the wedding date set on the calendar, and arrange for the wedding rehearsal early.

2. A minimum of one counseling interview between bride/groom and pastor is required soon after the wedding date is set.

More counseling interviews will be determined by the Pastor.

3. Arrangements should be made with the Church Secretary to make sure the wedding date is on the church calendar and obtain more information about the church usage policy.

4. The Pastor shall be in complete charge of all wedding proceedings in the Sanctuary, including the rehearsal.

5. The Pastor must be consulted ahead of time about the usage of cameras, decorations, etc.

6. In light of world hunger, the Trustees discourage the practice of throwing rice (bird seed is permitted).

It is only natural that certain costs are involved.

The following is a schedule of necessary charges. These should be <u>paid in advance</u> (before the day of rehearsal) when the bride and groom bring the license to the church office.

Minimum Honoraria:

    Minister: $

    Custodian: Check with the Pastor or Trustees

    Organist: Check with the Organist

(Revised Date:_____)

Sample Application for Use of Church Facilities

Date of Application:

Name of the Organization and/or Individual Applying:
(The applicant is responsible for payment, supervision, setting up, clean-up, damage, etc.)
Address:
Telephone:
Fax:

Date and Time You Plan to Use the Facilities:

Do you plan to Use the Facilities on a Regular Basis? If so,

Once ( )   Weekly ( )   Monthly ( )   Annually ( )

Hours of Active Use:
Specify Purpose:

Please indicate type of room(s) requested: (Please Circle)
Fellowship Hall, Kitchen, Classroom (how many?)_____, Other
Equipment Needed: Chairs, Tables, etc.

Person Responsible for Payment
   Name:
   Address:
   Tax ID # (if applicable):

Advance Payment:
Special Request, if any:

Check should be made payable to:
. . . United Methodist Church
Any Town, USA 000000

_____

FOR OFFICE USE ONLY:
DATE:
APPROVED: TITLE:
DISAPPROVED: TITLE:
(ADDITIONAL CHARGES FOR CUSTODIAL SERVICES MAY BE DETERMINED
BY TRUSTEES).
(AN ADVANCE DEPOSIT IS REQUIRED DURING THE TIME OF
RESERVATION FOR NON-MEMBERS)

SAMPLE PERSONNEL POLICIES AND
PROCEDURES MANUAL

For Staff Members of This United Methodist Church[2]
Revised Date: _____

The Purpose of This Manual

The purpose of this manual is to provide each staff member with the personnel poli-cies of the ... United Methodist Church. The ... United Methodist Church complies with the employment policy of the local and federal governments and the guideline provided in *The Book of Discipline*. As a body of Christ, the local church hires, pro-motes, and retires staff members in a manner consistent with the commitment of The United Methodist Church to ethnic, racial, and sexual inclusiveness without discrim-ination on the basis of race, age, sex, or handicapping situations. Therefore this church shall:

a) recruit, employ, utilize, recompense, and promote their professional staff and other personnel in a manner consistent with the commitment of The ... United Methodist Church to ethnic, racial, and sexual inclusiveness.

b) fulfill their duties and responsibilities in a manner which does not involve segrega-tion or discrimination on the basis of race, age, sex, or handicapping conditions.

Staff members who are not under episcopal appointment in The ... United Methodist Church are employed based on their qualifications to perform their tasks and their commitment to their work as described by the Staff-Parish Relations Committee (from now on referred to as Committee). Copies of current job descrip-tions are retained in the files maintained by the Committee, Pastor, and church office. The job descriptions are kept as part of the annual performance review done by the Committee.

We sincerely hope that the execution of these rules and regulations will foster understanding, fair administration, and standardization of procedure.

All staff members are expected to maintain a high moral and ethical standard as they give human face to the ministries of the church. Violations of the rules and infringements of the regulations will be sufficient grounds for disciplinary action.

General Administration

The Pastor of the congregation serves as the Administrative Officer of the church as outlined in *The Book of Discipline*. The Pastor administers the church's programs within goals and policies set by the Church Conference and/or Administrative Council; represents the Council to the church and to the community; and provides leadership to the local church and its staff.

Employment and Orientation

After the new employee is appointed by the Staff-Parish Relations Committee, the employee should report to the Pastor of the church for a general orientation, enrollment in benefit programs (if applicable), and the completion and processing of all vital information forms necessary for placement in the payroll system. The Pastor will also answer the questions the new employee may have.

Induction and Orientation

At the time a person is employed, the Pastor will review with him or her the general policies of the ... United Methodist Church. The Pastor will orient the new employee on the work and the role of the staff as outlined in the job description and consistent with *The Book of Discipline*. The Pastor will give special orientation about the importance of maintaining confidentiality in office matters.

Health Examination and Background Check

As a condition of employment, all new staff members are required to submit an up-to-date health certificate obtained from a doctor. Upon receipt of satisfactory results from the doctor, the Committee will seal the document and keep it in a CONFIDENTIAL file.

All staff members are also expected to go through the background and credit check.

Working Conditions

Staff members are expected to be neatly and appropriately dressed and groomed at all times during work time. Inappropriate business (office) attire will not be permitted. Each employee is expected to use careful judgment in choosing his or her attire. For more detailed information, contact the Pastor or the Staff-Parish Relations Committee.

Staff members are expected and required to report to work in appropriate mental and physical conditions. It is the church's intent and obligation to provide a drug-free, healthful, safe, and secure work environment.

Sexual and racial harassment are not tolerated in the church's work place.

The unlawful manufacture, distribution, dispensation, possession, or use of alcohol and/or illegal drugs on the church's premises are absolutely prohibited. Violation of this policy will result in disciplinary action up to and including discharge, and may have legal consequences. Any suspicious object or activity found on church facilities should be reported immediately to the Pastor and/or the Trustees.

The Trustees of the church take all precautions to furnish employees with a work setting free from recognized hazards that might cause serious injury or death. The Trustees take every possible measure to comply with the specific safety and health standards issued by the Health and Labor Department.

Therefore, it is the responsibility of the employee to comply with safety and health standards, rules, and regulations. Each employee is obligated to immediately report safety and health hazards to the Pastor and the Trustees.

Presence of Family Members on Premises

Unless it is necessary, the Committee discourages staff members from bringing family members to the work place.

It is also unfair to subject co-workers to the disruption caused by children in the work place. Additionally, the church could face possible liability if the child of the staff becomes sick or is injured while at the church's offices.

Except for a brief and occasional visit, staff members are advised not to bring their spouses or family members to the work place. Telephone calls to family and friends during work time are highly discouraged.

Receiving phone calls from family and friends, except on emergency situations, should be absolutely avoided.

No personal/family business can be transacted during work time nor from within the church premises.

Friends and family members of the staff or Pastor are strictly prohibited from using office equipment.

Listening to music, radio, news, or watching video or TV during work time is strictly forbidden.

Employees who have to leave their work place or change their time schedule should first consult with the Pastor. Any permanent change has to be approved by the Committee.

Church and Staff members are not permitted to use the copier machine to make photocopies for personal purposes. Copies that need to be made for ecumenical and community events should be cleared with the Pastor. There is a subsidized charge for all community programs. (Five cents for non-profit charity and ecumenical programs. Ten cents for personal copies, per page).

Pay Day

Salary checks are distributed on the second and fourth Thursday of each month.

Automatic Payroll Deposit may be arranged through the Treasurer/Financial Secretary of the Church. In that case, the salary check will be deposited directly to the staff's checking account. Upon termination of services (resignation/termination) from the church, automatic payroll will be stopped.

Salary Advance

No advance salary is paid under any circumstances.

Salary Withholding by the Employer

The employee's share of Social Security, federal, state, and city income taxes are withheld by the Treasurer.

Holidays

A list of holidays will be circulated after the Charge Conference, for the following calendar year. The holidays are set by the Staff-Parish Relations Committee, in consultation with the Pastor. Some holidays will vary from year to year. The number of holidays are set by the good will of the Staff-Parish Relations Committee. The Committee may decrease the number of holidays as and when necessary.

Unless the office is officially closed by the Pastor or by the Committee, all employees are expected to be in their work place. Employees who fail to get to work because of inclement weather, road repairs, etc. will have to use available vacation leave.

No make-up time or compensation days are allowed.

Sick Leave

Sick leave is granted only by the approval of the Staff-Parish Relations Committee. Under no circumstance will more than four weeks of sick leave be granted.

Vacation

No paid vacation is granted for staff members who work less than full-time. No personal leave is granted for part-time employees.

Staff members who are qualified for vacation are allowed to accrue their vacation time. However, only one week of accrued vacation is permitted to be carried over to the following year. No cash remuneration will be given for lost vacation.

Overtime

No overtime work is permitted. If an employee does not show up to work because of inclement weather or vehicular or personal problems, the lost time or day cannot be automatically made up another day or week. The lost hour/day/days will be taken out of the employee's vacation or holidays.

Voluntary Termination

A written notice of at least <u>two weeks</u> prior to the anticipated effective date of resignation is expected of the full-time staff. Failure to do so will result in losing two weeks of salary.

Involuntary Termination

General Comments
Abolition of a position because of reorganization, contraction of program, or reduced funds may result in termination of services of a part-time or full-time staff person who is performing satisfactorily. The Committee will notify the staff about the procedures

and the process. It is absolutely up to the decision of the Committee, in consultation with the Pastor, to set the hiring and retiring policy of the church in accordance with *The Book of Discipline* of The United Methodist Church.

Mandatory Retirement
The mandatory retirement of all employees is the 70th birthday. No exceptions will be entertained.

Disciplinary Procedures
The Staff-Parish Relations Committee of the ... United Methodist Church reserves the right to exercise disciplinary action for consistently poor job performance, inappropriate conduct, extreme tardiness, or behavior contrary to the mission and ministries of the congregation. This action may take the form of verbal reprimand, written reprimand, probation, suspension, or termination.

Termination of services for unsatisfactory performance or breach of confidentiality may be initiated by the Pastor or Staff-Parish Relations Committee.

A staff member may be suspended and/or terminated for continued poor job performance, improper conduct, excessive tardiness, or behavior contrary to the mission and ministries of the congregation.

Personal Telephone Calls

The church's telephones are for business use only. However, the church recognizes there may be a necessity to make or receive a limited number of personal telephone calls. Personal calls are to be paid for by the employee. The cost is thirty cents for each local call. The long distance calls are charged as per the billing.

Frequent reception of phone calls from friends and family for personal matters is strictly prohibited.

Lost and Found Articles

The church is not responsible for personal property lost or stolen on church premises. Lost or found articles should be reported to the Pastor and/or Trustees. Every effort will be made to locate and return such articles to their rightful owners.

Security

All doors that can be locked should be when the last person leaves for the day. The doors are, generally, unlocked at 7:50 a.m. and secured at 4:00 p.m. Individual access

to offices at other times should be discussed with the Pastor/Secretary.
If any equipment or personal property should be missing, the Pastor and Trustees
should be notified immediately.

Smoking

Smoking is prohibited on church premises.

Travel Expenses

Staff traveling in the service of the church are reimbursed after the approval of the
Pastor and the Staff-Parish Relations Committee. No travel should be undertaken
without the prior approval of the Staff-Parish Relations Committee. Failure to do so
will result in forfeiting the reimbursement.

Work Rules

The purpose of these rules and regulations is to define and protect the rights of all; it
is not meant to restrict the rights of anyone. It is hoped that the implementation of
these rules and regulations will promote understanding, even-handed administration
and uniformity of procedure. All employees are expected to maintain a high standard
of conduct and work performance. Infractions of the rules and regulations will be sufficient grounds for disciplinary action ranging from reprimand to immediate discharge
depending upon the seriousness and frequency of the infractions. Violations of two or
more of the work rules in Class I and/or Class II during any twelve-month period of
time may result in immediate discharge.

The following are not intended to be all-inclusive
Subject to a Penalty from Reprimand to Discharge

Class I Violations
The following is a partial list of improper conduct which, when engaged in, shall constitute grounds for disciplinary action including discharge:
1. Absence from work without authorization of the Pastor or the Staff-Parish Relations
Committee.
2. Stealing or sabotage of equipment, tools, or other property belonging to the church
or to any congregation member.
3. Misuse or removal from the church's premises of any church's property or property
of others without permission from the Pastor or Trustees.
4. Dishonesty, including any falsification or misrepresentation; providing incomplete,
misleading, or incorrect information in connection with the preparation or handling
of church's records, including an application for employment.

5. Willful damage, abuse, or destruction of church's property or the property of others.

6. Working against the recommendations or decisions made by the Staff-Parish Relations Committee or the Administrative Council or any other committee's recommendations which were communicated to the employee.

7. Possession, sale, or use of intoxicating beverages or drugs on church's property or reporting for work under the influence of intoxicating beverages or drugs.

8. Unauthorized use, possession, conveyance, or storage of any firearms, explosives, or other dangerous weapons on church's premises or during church's time.

9. Insubordination, including refusal to perform work required by the Pastor.

10. Use of profane, abusive, threatening language toward fellow employees, visitors, and church members.

11. Fighting, intimidating, coercing, interfering with, or threatening bodily injury to other employees, visitors, guests, and church members.

12. Gambling of any kind on the church's premises.

13. Any act which might endanger the safety or life of others.

14. Willful, deliberate, or repeated violation of safety rules.

15. Deliberately delaying or restricting services or work effort, or inciting others to delay or confuse, or restrict same.

16. Failure to report to work upon expiration of a vacation, holiday, or leave of absence.

17. Disclosure of confidential church information.

18. Unauthorized use of church money, telephones, stationery, church's name, property, or equipment.

Class II Violations
Prior Warning Before Disciplinary Action Such as Suspension or Discharge

The following is a partial list of improper conduct which when engaged in, shall constitute grounds for issuance of a warning before severe disciplinary action is taken up to and including discharge:

1. Engaging in any activity that endangers others, interferes with work, or creates a non-work environment.

2. Carelessness or recklessness causing damage to, defacement of, or destruction of building, equipment, or other church property or the property of church members and visitors.

3. Unsatisfactory work performance.

4. Excessive tardiness.

5. Solicitation or collecting contributions by an employee during work time and distribution of literature in working areas at any time.

6. Leaving regularly assigned work location without notifying the Pastor.

7. Creating or contributing to unsanitary, or otherwise poor, housekeeping conditions.

8. Failure to observe working hour schedule, starting or quitting times, and/or rest or meal hours.

9. Interfering with any employee's performance of duties by talking or causing other distractions.

10. Performing unauthorized personal work on church's time.

Sexual Harassment Policy

The ... United Methodist Church will neither condone nor tolerate harassment of one employee by another including derogatory remarks, racial or ethnic innuendos, sexual harassment, or any activity which tends to defame, ridicule, intimidate, or embarrass an employee. Sexual harassment is defined as any unwanted sexual advances or demands (verbal or physical) which are perceived by the recipient as demeaning, intimidating, or coercive.

Employees are expected to discipline their verbal and physical expression in interpersonal relationships to avoid the appearance of questionable motivation or disregard for individual sensitivities.

Employees alleging harassment should report the occurrence to the Pastor, the Staff-Parish Relations Committee, or the Administrative Council. The church's policy is to maintain a working environment conducive to the full humanity of all its employees. It will also include counseling with the employee charged with the harassment and continued follow-up on his or her behavior. Continued inappropriate behavior may result in suspension or termination.

Complaints will be handled confidentially in order to protect the rights of the complainant, the accused, and persons who may serve as witnesses, and to ensure against retaliation or intimidation.

Notes

1. These forms are suggestions only.
2. This is meant to be a sample only. Please read and edit to fit the circumstances of your church.

SELECTED BIBLIOGRAPHY

Adams, Maurianne, Lee Anne Bell, and Pat Griffin, eds. *Teaching for Diversity and Social Justice*. New York: Routledge, 1997.

Crosby, Philip. *Quality Is Free*. New York: McGraw Hill, 1979.

Gonzalez, Justo. *The Changing Shape of Church History*. St. Louis, Missouri: Chalice Press, 2002.

Haas, Irene. *A Summertime Song*. New York: Margaret K. McElderberry Books, 1998.

Jenney, Ray Freeman. *Speaking Boldly: Essay-Sermons*. New York: Revell, 1935.

Kawasaki, Guy. *Rules of Revolutionaries*. New York: Harper and Row, 1959.

Kim, Young-Il, ed. *Knowledge, Attitude, and Experience [Ministry in the Cross-Cultural Context]*. Nashville: Abingdon Press, 1992.

Kiline, Peter, and Bernard Saunders. *To a Learning Organization*. Arlington, Va.: Great Ocean Publishers, 1993.

McClendon, James William, Jr. *Witness* [Systematic Theology Volume 3]. Nashville: Abingdon Press, 2000.

McSpadden, Lucia Ann. *Meeting God at the Boundaries*. Nashville: General Board of Higher Education and Ministry, 2003.

Nelson, Shirley. *The Last Year of the War*. New York: Harper and Row, 1978.

Recinos, Harold J. *Who Comes in the Name of the Lord?* Nashville: Abingdon Press, 1997.

Thurman, Howard. *With Head and Heart*. New York: Harcourt Brace Jovanovich, 1979.

_____. *The Luminous Darkness*. New York: Harper & Row,1965.

_____. *The Search for Common Ground*. New York: Harper & Row Publisher, 1971.

Breinigsville, PA USA
29 March 2010
235123BV00003B/7/P